NATURE ON SANIBEL

By
Margaret H. Greenberg

Illustrations by Steven R. Phillips
Photographs and Cover by David Meardon

ANNA PUBLISHING, INC., OCOEE, FLORIDA 32761

© Copyright 1985 by
Margaret H. Greenberg
P.O. Box 170
Sanibel Island, Florida 33957

Library of Congress
Catalog Card Number: 85-72242

International Standard Book Number: 0-89305-060-1

Printed in the U.S.A.

ANNA PUBLISHING, INC., OCOEE, FLORIDA 32761

TABLE OF CONTENTS

PART V: BIRDS OF MANY FEATHERS

PART VI: GUARDIANS OF THE SANCTUARY ISLAND

To Maxene B. Michl,

for suggesting that I write this book,
and putting up with me while I did.

ACKNOWLEDGMENTS

While I hope that readers will find this book to be an original and lively introduction to nature on Sanibel, the factual information that it contains could not possibly have been derived from the experiences and observations of a single individual. Therefore, I am grateful for the opportunity to acknowledge, both here and in the bibliography, those scientists and naturalists whose fine work was of inestimable value in terms of my own research.

Any writer who seeks to condense a wealth of diverse information, often highly technical, into layman's language runs the very real risk of allowing a felicitous phrase to wreak havoc with scientific precision! Thus I am particularly indebted to several island naturalists, who graciously agreed to provide critical readings of the text prior to publication. The corrections and suggestions of Griffing Bancroft, Arthur Clark and Steve Phillips were instrumental in ensuring the accuracy of *Nature on Sanibel*.

Although illustrators rarely receive much credit for their work, apart from seeing their names in small print on the title page, *Nature on Sanibel* is considerably enhanced by the fine illustrations of Steven R. Phillips, and by the lovely color photographs of David Meardon. In addition to acknowledging the important contribution of their respective talents, I should like to thank David for waiting so patiently for the Royal Poinciana to bloom, and Steve for indulging my aversion for his beloved snakes!

M.H.G.

FOREWORD

According to the dictionary, a naturalist is simply someone who studies Nature. Thus it is both fair and accurate to say that this book was written by an amateur naturalist for the benefit of those who would like to know something (but for heaven's sake not too much!) about Sanibel's incredible variety of plant and animal life.

Since this tiny barrier island is virtually teeming with hundreds of species of plants and wildlife, the neophyte naturalist may well be overwhelmed, if not downright intimidated, by the number of white birds of different species, the plethora of native plants that all appear to be green, *etc.* Moreover, those who persevere and purchase authoritative books frequently find that their authors are unduly enamored of impenetrable scientific jargon, liberally laced with Latin.

Thus the main purpose of *Nature on Sanibel* is to provide an introduction to the flora and fauna that one is most likely to see on this island. Since all the species under discussion are extremely interesting, and many are rather amusing as well, I have tried to portray those characteristics in layman's language that favors the humorous over the ponderous. Although the Latin nomenclature for native plants is indicated below their common names, that temporary lapse into scientific technicality is solely due to the fact that so many of our indigenous species have several common names!

Every year, several hundred thousand people come to Sanibel in order to enjoy tropical sun, gentle surf, beautiful beaches, thousands of shells, and fine opportunities for golf and tennis. I hope that readers of *Nature on Sanibel* will also come to enjoy the extraordinary opportunity to observe all manner of plant and animal life in their natural habitats, feel greatly enriched by that experience, and be moved to support efforts to conserve and preserve Nature's bounty for the benefit and enjoyment of future generations.

In the final analysis, an Islander is not just a permanent Sanibel resident. Rather, a true Islander is *anyone* who loves this island and wants to retain the delicate balance between its two major attractions: vacation haven and wildlife sanctuary.

7

Margaret H. Greenberg
Sanibel Island

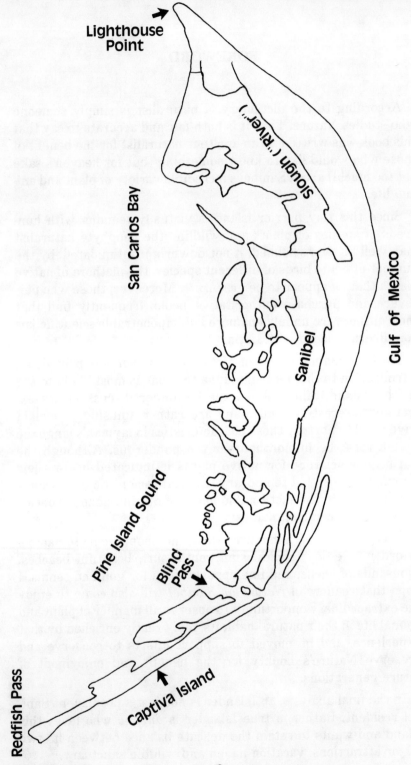

Lighthouse Point

San Carlos Bay

Slough ("River")

Gulf of Mexico

Sanibel

Pine Island Sound

Blind Pass

Captiva Island

Redfish Pass

8

CHAPTER 1.

FROM SAND BAR TO SANIBEL

From Maine to Texas, some 300 offshore islands of various shapes and sizes protect the coasts of the Atlantic and Gulf states. Such barrier islands are the mainland's first and last defense against the awesome onslaught of the very forces that created most of them in the first place: howling winds, raging storms, and devastating hurricanes.

Although the nation's largest peninsula braves the elements from the Atlantic Ocean, the Gulf of Mexico, and the Straits of Florida, Nature has blessed her bold creation with about 80 barrier islands. Thus beneath all the concrete, cheek-by-jowl condominiums and urban trappings lies a barrier island known as Miami Beach!

Fortunately, not all of Florida's barrier islands look like Miami Beach. However, only Sanibel is unique, a distinction that is partly due to a geographical peculiarity. With the exception of Sanibel, all of Florida's barrier islands (including Captiva), lie parallel to the coast and have a north-south orientation.

While Sanibel initially conformed to that typical pattern in the Wulfert Point area, it subsequently curved like an archer's bow, perhaps due to pressure from the water expelled by the Caloosahatchee River. In any event, Sanibel's unique east-west orientation is primarily responsible for its claim to fame as "the shell capital of the world." In effect, the island's Gulf-side shoreline is like a 12-mile net that ensnares some 400 species of shells stirred up by stormy seas.

REFLECTIONS ON AN OFFSHORE SAND BAR

Since most of Sanibel's resort accommodations are situated along the Gulf of Mexico, one can swim or wade to the first offshore sand bar in no time at all, the form of propulsion being entirely dependent upon the tides. Having arrived at the sand bar, many visitors feel compelled to pause and admire the beauty of the island that they have barely left behind, marvel at the pelican's ability to crash land on the water without breaking all its bones in the process, or just thank God that they are wallowing in the Gulf of Mexico and not shoveling snow in Ohio! Thus reaching the first sand bar is an ineffable experience that causes human preoccupations and problems to pale by comparison.

Thousands of years ago, Sanibel Island was much like that first sand bar, an offshore spit of sand that was briefly exposed at low tide and quickly reclaimed by the sea. Gradually, however, storms and turbulent waters deposited more and more sand and shells, with the result that this "gift from the sea" no longer vanished at high tide. Thus about 5,000 years ago, the small mass of sand, shells and crushed rocks was ready to receive its first pioneer, a remarkable tree that would help transform a sand bar into an island that is now called Sanibel.

MANGROVE SEEDLING

THE MIRACLE OF THE MANGROVES

In crossing the Causeway, one has a magnificent view of a vast forest of mangroves guarding the shores of San Carlos Bay and Pine Island Sound. Those silent sentinels are Red Mangroves, descendants of the pioneer seedlings that first established a foothold on this sand bar around 3,000 B.C. Not at all impressive in terms of appearance, and often called "green cigars," the 8″ seedlings are instrumental in building islands out of shifting sands and protecting their vulnerable creations from the elements.

Once dropped into the water, Red Mangrove seedlings may drift for many months and hundreds of miles before landing on an exposed spit of sand and taking root, their vitality quite unimpaired by the long ocean voyage. On the other hand, some seedlings settle near the parent tree, while others float for a few miles before coming to rest on an offshore sand bar.

Whether the distance from the parent tree be measured in inches or in miles, a Red Mangrove seedling will invariably do three things in very short order: sink roots into the sand, send leaf shoots up into the air, and support its fledgling stem (and future trunk) with a series of prop roots that would certainly rival the flying buttresses of any medieval cathedral. Should several seedlings anchor on the same sand bar, their prop roots will eventually form an impenetrable jungle, and a new island.

One might well wonder how any tree could possibly survive and prosper in a salt-water environment! Indeed, few can. However, the roots of the Red Mangrove are equipped with special membranes that prevent salt from seeping into the tree. On those rare occasions when the membranes prove inadequate to their assigned task, the tree donates a few sacrificial leaves to the debris around its roots. For the most part, however, the Red Mangrove survives, thrives, builds up the land, and thus eventually provides a hospitable home for a vast variety of plants and animals.

Once a group of Red Mangrove seedlings becomes established on a sand bar, all kinds of things collect around their prop roots, thereby forming new land and building an island out of sand, shells, decayed vegetation, and a wide assortment of debris.

11

While Red Mangroves made possible the transformation of an offshore sand bar into Sanibel, other forces have always shaped the destinies of fragile barrier islands.

Storms, winds, and tides along the Gulf are constantly altering the shoreline, with the result that some property owners lose their beach while others gain more than they ever had before. The great hurricane of 1926 sliced through Captiva and created Redfish Pass, thereby separating Upper Captiva from its larger sibling. Moreover, storms are forever opening and closing Blind Pass between Sanibel and Captiva. Thus "the more things change, the more they remain the same" is an adage that could never apply to Sanibel, or to any other barrier island.

MORE PLANTS ARRIVE

Since islands are completely surrounded by water, one has to wonder how such an astonishing variety of flora and fauna ever managed to arrive on Sanibel. In this connection, plants are especially puzzling. After all, any first grader knows perfectly well that plants do not fly or swim. And yet, much of Sanibel's native vegetation arrived (and continues to arrive) by air, by bird, and by water! Fortunately, there is a very logical explanation for such a phenomenon, if one banishes incredible visions of flying or swimming shrubs and trees and thinks in terms of spores and seeds.

The spores of the very simplest forms of flora stand the best chance of being blown thither and yon by the wind. Thus a host of algae, fungi, ferns and their relatives arrived on Sanibel courtesy of the prevailing winds. While seed-producing plants might appear to be less promising candidates for distant dispersal, some seeds are equipped with special devices that catch the wind.

Although seeds that lack such devices are probably too heavy to soar like gliders in the air, many are actually *flown* to their unknown destinations by birds. Since birds love berries, but are not always able to digest their seeds, the latter are dropped willy-nilly whenever a bird feels the urge to jettison its undigested cargo. Thus the Strangler Fig frequently finds a hospitable home in the petioles of a Cabbage Palm.

In addition to free rides by air and by bird, a few of Sanibel's native plants arrived with the incoming tides. As indicated earlier, the pioneer Red Mangrove seedlings are able to survive a long, salt-water voyage without ill effects. The Coconut Palm and several species of Morning Glory are also endowed with the ability to float for extended periods without diminution of vitality upon arrival.

THE ARRIVAL OF ANIMALS

Like plants, animals also arrived (and continue to arrive) by air, by bird, and by water. Obviously, the presence of birds on an offshore island is not the least bit peculiar. In addition to flying in the undigested cargo of plant seeds, however, birds brought a variety of insect eggs encased in mud on their feathers and legs.

A number of animals, like alligators and otters, simply swam from the mainland, perhaps stopping to rest at some of the little mangrove islands in the bay that are such convenient stepping stones to Sanibel. Many other species also arrived by water, perched precariously on palm fronds or on mainland trees dislodged by storms.

Thus for several thousand years, hundreds of species of plants and animals from microscopic spores to 17-foot alligators have found a home on Sanibel. The fact that such an incredible variety of vegetation and wildlife not only survived but indeed thrived on this barrier island is largely due to the presence of two, totally different environments: the salt-water nursery of the bay and the fresh-water wetlands of the interior.

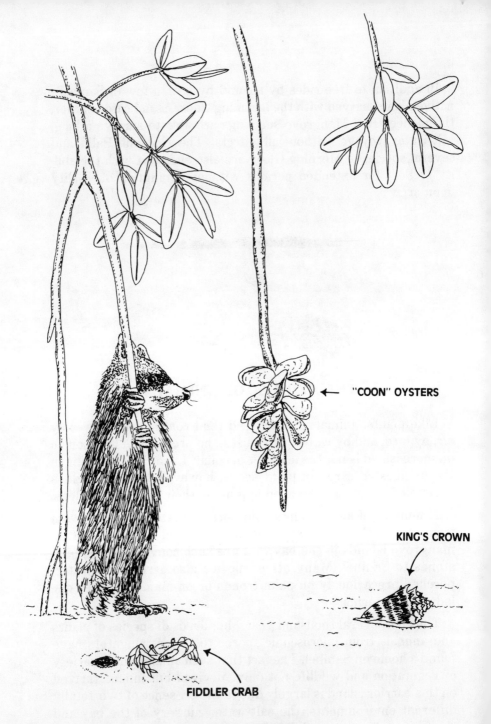

"COON" OYSTERS

KING'S CROWN

FIDDLER CRAB

LIFE AROUND MANGROVE

14

CHAPTER 2.

WATER, WATER EVERYWHERE

NURSERIES OF THE PLANET EARTH

Since all barrier islands are separated from the mainland by bays, there is nothing unusual about the presence of Pine Island Sound and San Carlos Bay. However, Kristie Seaman, a marine biologist at the J.N. "Ding" Darling National Wildlife Refuge, cites a staggering statistic: about 70 percent of all ocean fish begin their lives in such sheltered bay areas! Moreover, bays are vast nurseries for an astonishing variety of other living things as well, and are thus indispensable for the continuation of that complex ecological chain known as life on earth.

Obviously, a discussion of life on earth is a topic of monumental proportions that defies the confines of a single book, and most certainly exceeds the capacities of this author. However, a brief consideration of several forms of life that are supported or nurtured by the pioneer Red Mangrove trees provides a fine introduction to the critical importance of salt-water bays.

Thanks to the presence of a narrow wooden footbridge at Stop No. 4 in the "Ding" Darling Refuge, one can observe a great deal of wildlife without sinking into the muck while brandishing a machete in order to clear a path. Before crossing that footbridge, however, visitors may be entertained by the busy activities of the Fiddler Crab, one of the most conspicuous creatures of the salt marsh. At low tide, entire colonies of those little crustaceans (about 1″ wide) scurry sideways across the mud in search of tiny organic morsels.

The Fiddler Crab derives its name from the fact that one of the male's claws is considerably larger than the other and bears some resemblance to a violin or fiddle. The larger claw is generally used to fend off other males in mating-season battles, or to lure female Fiddlers into the burrow with a distinct "come hither" gesture. Apart from those antics, however, flailing away with the larger claw is primarily an exercise in intimidation and little more than a bluff.

When faced with real danger, the Fiddler Crab is quick to make a beeline for its burrow, a feat of crab engineering that may be 3' long. Before condemning the Fiddler Crab for cowardice, however, one should consider the fact that its burrowing propensities constantly bring nutrient particles below the mud to the surface. Thus be it comical or cowardly, the tiny Fiddler Crab plays a vital role in the ecology of the marsh.

Many people consider the salt marshes at the edge of mud flats to be malodorous wastelands. However, a short walk to the platform at the end of the footbridge will surely convince anyone that such areas are among the richest wildlife communities on earth. En route, one is surrounded by a seemingly impenetrable jungle of Red Mangroves, their prop roots coated with algae and encrusted with barnacles, mussels, snails and "coon" oysters, all of which seem to find the slimy coating of algae quite delectable.

Fish hunt in the offshore cordgrasses at high tide, while low tide brings a host of invaders from the land: snakes, turtles, rabbits, otters, raccoons, a large variety of birds, and swarms of insects. An ibis may poke its curved beak among the floating stew of algae in search of tasty morsels hiding under the greenery, while raccoons endowed with incredible dexterity pry open a "coon" oyster (much to the dismay of the ravenous King's Crown snail that also preys upon such delicacies). No wonder raccoons are able to remove the lids of just about any garbage can devised by man!

Further evidence of the critical importance of bays lies just a short distance away from the platform at Stop No. 4: the series of little mangrove islands that dot the waters of San Carlos Bay. Such islands are the preferred nesting areas of the endangered Brown Pelican and a variety of egrets, herons and ibises. Surrounded by water, the rookeries are relatively safe from the invasion of predators that prefer to prowl for prey that is accessible by land.

THE WETLANDS

Sanibel has two, low beach ridges that are approximately 4-7' above sea level. The Sanibel-Captiva Road follows the general outline of the northern, bay-side ridge, while the southern ridge runs roughly parallel to the famous shelling beaches along the Gulf of Mexico. Never more than 3' above sea level, the fresh-water wetlands of the swales lie between those main beach ridges. Although the water is really more brackish than fresh, it is vital to the survival of a remarkable variety of vegetation and wildlife.

Actually, the presence of fresh-water wetlands on an offshore island is not so unusual. Other barrier islands once had such interior wetlands, although many have now lost them to draining and filling for development. What makes Sanibel unique, however, is the existence of *two* fresh-water systems: the visible wetlands of the swales *on* the land, and the invisible lens of fresh water lying just a few feet *under* the land. Although seemingly separate, the two systems are mutually dependent.

One of the most important functions of the shallow, fresh-water system underlying much of the island is to prevent the intrusion of salt water into the wetlands. In return for services rendered, fresh water from the wetlands of the swales seeps down into the underground lens, thereby replenishing that system. The amount of water in the swales is, of course, entirely dependent upon the amount of rainfall. On Sanibel, the "rainy season" normally occurs during the hot summer months, when bugs are far more prevalent than people!

THE MYTH OF THE SANIBEL RIVER

Any map of Sanibel printed within the last twenty years will show a thin ribbon of water between Chateau-sur-Mer and Beach Road, surely a unique geographical feature on a barrier island! About 8 miles long as the Fish Crow flies, or some 15 miles of watery twists and turns by canoe, nearly everyone calls this serpentine waterway the Sanibel River. Although there really is no river on Sanibel, only a few remember the slough.

The fleeting reference to "bugs" at the end of the preceding section has a great deal to do with the myth of the Sanibel River.

Prior to the early 1960s, the natural swales of the wetlands were called the Sanibel Slough. Unfortunately, mosquitoes found the sere, cracked mud of the slough to be a most delightful breeding area during the dry season. Although Sanibel was proud to be known as "the shell capital of the world," the fact that it was also referred to as "the mosquito capital of the world" was not at all flattering. Moreover, so far as residents and off-season visitors were concerned, life in an insect Eden was utterly intolerable!

Islanders used to keep palm fronds by their doors in order to flail away at the millions of mosquitoes that blackened the screens in eager anticipation of the arrivals and departures of *Homo sapiens*. Since some 400,000 were once caught in a single light trap one night, Sanibel may hold the world's most unwanted record! Clearly something had to be done, and thus the taming of the slough resulted in that man-made waterway that is now called the Sanibel River.

Lee County Mosquito Control undertook a massive project that involved dredging, widening, and permanently connecting the main swales of the Sanibel Slough, thereby creating what is now called the Sanibel River. Thus today's "river" really has no source other than rainwater, and no final destination apart from the man-made sluices along San Carlos Bay.

SANIBEL'S MAN-MADE CANALS AND LAKES

Lee County Mosquito Control was also responsible for carving out Sanibel's labyrinth of canals, albeit not for the benefit of boaters. Rather, their purpose was to put gambusia and mollies into such brackish waters, since those tiny fish are particularly partial to mosquito larvae. Moreover, it was Mosquito Control that constructed a dike in "Ding" Darling in order to impound brackish water and introduce the little larvae-eating fish on the left side of what is now called Wildlife Drive.

In addition to including a "river" and a veritable maze of man-made canals, any map of modern Sanibel will also indicate the presence of several fresh-water lakes. While none of the preced-

18

ing are natural bodies of fresh or brackish water, the creation of artificial lakes had, for once, nothing to do with controlling the appalling population of insect vampires.

For the most part, developers dug out lakes in order to obtain fill for the purpose of increasing the elevation of their building lots. Needless to say, elevation is essential for the residents of a barrier island that is at the mercy of hurricanes and severe flooding. In addition to benefiting from the safety and slightly lower insurance rates of greater elevation, however, those who live along the shore of Sanibel's man-made lakes are privileged to enjoy a variety of wildlife that makes no picayune distinctions between natural and artificial water habitats.

THE ANCIENT ALLIGATOR HOLE

As indicated in the preceding sections, all bodies of fresh water that appear on maps of Sanibel are now permanent geographical features, but not natural ones. However, there *is* a body of fresh water that is both natural and permanent: the ancient alligator hole.

The alligator hole is located on the main tract of the Conservation Foundation at the end of the Sabal Palm Trail, and one may often see a gator in residence. Although a footbridge and observation platform have been constructed for the benefit and safety of visitors, the fresh-water pond has remained essentially untouched by Man for hundreds of years. Moreover, it serves as a reminder that alligators once performed a vital service for many other animals on Sanibel Island.

At certain times of the year, the old Sanibel Slough was a most unreliable source of fresh water for island wildlife. It often dried up completely and, as indicated earlier, was little more than a hospitable home for most unwelcome mosquitoes. Thus during the dry season, alligators saved many animals from certain death by digging down into the fresh-water lens and creating a water hole.

Quite understandably, alligators were motivated by primordial instincts for self-preservation and not the least bit inspired by

19

any form of animal altruism. They dug out ponds in order to immerse their bodies in the kind of water that would, among other things, keep their skin from drying up. The fact that many other animals were able to survive as a result of their efforts was of absolutely no interest to the alligators. However, should another creature linger too long at its fresh-water spa, a gator could hardly be blamed for administering the last rites!

Despite the fact that Sanibel will always have a dry season, our alligators are generally not obliged to exert themselves unduly by digging for fresh water. They are not purists when it comes to relatively fresh water, and are thus quite content to wallow in our man-made canals, lakes, golf course ponds, and even in the chlorinated pools of condominiums!

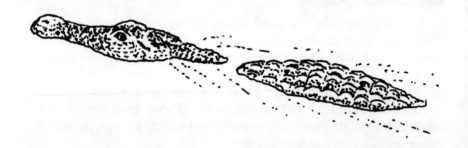

CHAPTER 3.

INTRODUCTION

Logic dictates that the neophyte naturalist begin with a study of island plants. However, the ardor for enlightenment may quickly be replaced by utter despair when one learns that some 250 native species are alive and well on Sanibel! Moreover, such a vague statistic gives rise to the sneaking suspicion that even more native vegetation may be lurking under the bushes, patiently awaiting proper scientific identification.

In addition to trying to cope with such a plethora of indigenous plants, the budding botanist is frequently frustrated in his efforts to distinguish one species from another for, quite frankly, Sanibel's native vegetation is overwhelmingly ever green and only green. Although a number of shrubs and trees produce colorful flowers and berries, the latter are generally called "inconspicuous." Furthermore, there is no guarantee that even the colorful "inconspicuous" will appear at that time of the year when one happens to be examining a particular specimen.

Fortunately, the Sanibel-Captiva Conservation Foundation has rescued countless Islanders and visitors from the quagmire of confusion. Its nature trails are always open to the public and, during the season, volunteer guides conduct several tours nearly every day. For quite a number of years, the Foundation has also offered a superb course to anyone who is interested in knowing more about Sanibel's plant and animal life.

Initially, it may be rather disconcerting to learn that the Australian Pine is neither a native nor a pine, that palm trees are not really trees, that Broom Sedge is a grass, Saw Grass is a sedge, and the Sea Grape bears no grapes! Moreover, as one Island friend innocently inquired when I was in the throes of studying native plants, "Doesn't everything still look all green and all the same to you?" Alas, I had to admit that, more often than not, it did.

However, one soon realizes that all those green leaves have very distinctive shapes and display the full gamut of green.

Moreover, they may appear shiny or rather dull, feel rough or as smooth as fine suede, and the species that they adorn may be armed with an awesome array of spines, prickles or thorns.

While admittedly not very colorful, the native plants of this barrier island are worthy of great respect for they are magnificent survivors. Unlike our introduced species, exotics, the natives are wonderfully energy efficient. They make few demands on natural resources, and almost none on the financial resources, time and energy of Sanibel's avid gardeners. They do not require chemical fertilizers (expensive and extremely harmful to the environment), nor do they need to be watered (thereby imposing a severe strain on a particularly precious resource that costs Islanders a small fortune).

In short, the remarkably salt-tolerant, energy-efficient, and extremely undemanding native species thrive on Sanibel simply because they belong here. Moreover, in addition to being peerless survivors, many of our indigenous plants have helped mankind in a variety of ways.

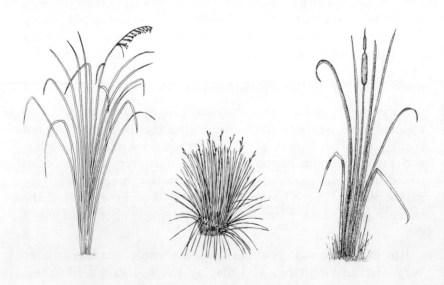

CHAPTER 4.

RAMPANT PLANTS ALONG THE RAMP

Native vegetation grows in great profusion all over Sanibel. Quite understandably, however, no signs identify the vast variety of green-leaved specimens that line our island roads. Thus both amateur naturalists and *bona fide* botanists may benefit from the fine introduction to native flora provided by the Sanibel-Captiva Conservation Foundation.

The Foundation's main, 207-acre tract is located on the Sanibel-Captiva Road, about one mile west of the Tarpon Bay Road intersection. Shortly after parking the car or bicycle, one walks up a gentle ramp that leads to the Center. Well over a dozen species line both sides of that wooden ramp, and all are clearly identified. Visitors may wish to linger a bit before entering the Center, for the great majority of those native plants along the ramp are the species that one most commonly sees on Sanibel.

WAX MYRTLE

WAX MYRTLE (SOUTHERN BAYBERRY)
Myrica cerifera

Wax Myrtle, the first labeled specimen on the right, is one of Sanibel's most prolific shrubs. It is invariably part of the dense foliage along the sides of many island roads where, undisturbed by Man's pruning propensities, it may reach a height of over 20 feet and look more like a tree than a modest shrub. Although its northern relative never attains such dizzy heights, both specimens have tiny green berries that are completely coated with a grayish wax.

Bayberries are the dietary delight of our migrating tree swallows and, for several centuries, Man has enjoyed the pleasant aroma of candles made from their waxy coating. Since bayberries are so tiny, about 1/8″ in diameter, one would probably have to boil many hundreds of them in order to skim off enough wax to make a single candle. After removing the wax, our ancestors often used the remaining gray-green liquid for dyeing their woolens, a practice that may explain why so many of our forebears look dreadfully dull and drab in paintings.

Since the rather vile-looking liquid was found to be very astringent, it was also used to shrink swollen gums and cure diarrhea. Bay leaves, of course, are still used in cooking. Although the leaves of our Wax Myrtle are not sold in stores, they may be substituted for the commercial product.

25

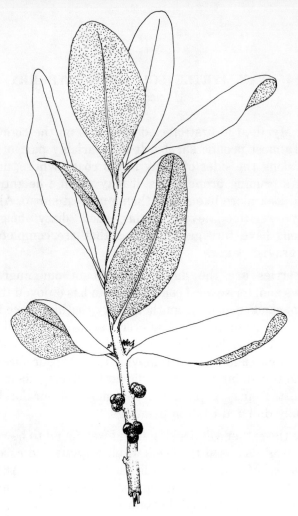

MYRSINE (RAPANEA)
Myrsine guianensis

Although Myrsine is generally called a shrub, it rivals Wax Myrtle in attaining tree-like heights. Indeed, the two species are often found growing side by side in many of the undeveloped, densely vegetated areas of the island.

The leaves, some 2-4″ long, are shiny and quite aromatic. When European explorers and traders introduced tobacco to Florida's Indians, many of the latter became quite addicted to it. Since tobacco was something of a luxury, however, the Indians often mixed it with Myrsine leaves in order to prolong the pleasure.

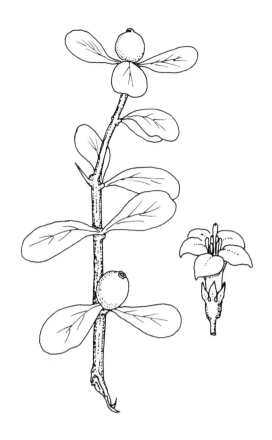

WHITE INDIGO BERRY
Randia aculeata

After passing a few more labeled specimens on the right, not without merit but not that common, one comes to the White Indigo Berry, a shrub that is generally armed with sharp spines at the ends of its branches. Although tiny white flowers bloom throughout the year, they are so small as to be inconspicuous. However, the berries from which this specimen derives its common name are of considerable interest. White on the outside and indigo on the inside, the Indians used their colorful pulp in making dye.

Having referred to Indians in connection with two of the three native species discussed so far, it is time to say a few introductory words about Sanibel's native Indians, the powerful Calusas who once dominated southern Florida.

THE CALUSA INDIANS

In 1513, Ponce de Leon accidentally discovered the east coast of what he called Florida when he was actually trying to find the fantasy island of Bimini that was supposed to have gold galore and, of particular interest to an over-the-hill conquistador, a fountain of youth. Although Ponce de Leon found hostile Indians rather than gold or eternal youth on Florida's east coast, he persevered, rounded the Keys, and eventually sailed into what is now called San Carlos Bay in honor of Carlos, the mighty chief of some 20,000 Calusa Indians.

Although Ponce de Leon's reception on the west coast of Florida was no less hostile than it had been on the east coast, he returned in 1521 with the intention of establishing a settlement at the mouth of the Caloosahatchee River. The Calusas attacked, a number of Spaniards were killed, and Ponce de Leon received what later proved to be a mortal wound in the form of a Calusa arrow in his thigh.

For the next 200 years or so, the Calusas were subjected to the guns and diseases of European conquerors, missionaries, slave hunters and traders. Their ranks decimated by diseases against which they had no immunity, and savagely reduced by slave hunters, a few thousand Calusas and other Indians made their last stand in 1712 on the island that is now called Key West. Thus when Ponce de Leon accidentally discovered Florida in 1513, the Calusas were at the height of their cultural and political dominance of the southern portion of that peninsula. 199 years later, those proud and powerful Indians were effectively extinct.

Much of what we know about the daily diet of the Calusa Indians is derived from Spanish records and from the hard, painstaking work of archaeologists who have studied many sites, including a number on Sanibel, Captiva, and other barrier islands in this general area. The shell mound on the Gasparilla Trail at the "Ding" Darling Refuge is but a small part of a much larger complex located on private property.

It appears that the Calusas were one of those rare exceptions to the rule that agriculture is essential to the establishment of a large and relatively settled society. Since the bounty from both land and sea provided tasty and reliable sustenance, the Calusas shopped freely in Nature's splendid supermarket and were never really obliged to work for a living! Thus they ate all manner of shellfish and many species of fish.

While killing land animals involved a bit more work, evidence from archaeological sites indicates that the Calusas consumed rats, rabbits, raccoons, snakes, birds and alligators. In addition, they made use of the fruits and berries of many native plants and ate "swamp cabbage" (hearts of palm). Since it is not always possible to determine precisely which native plants the Calusas included in their diet, any reference to Indians in connection with plants in this book means that the Calusas *may* have used the plant for food and, if not, other Florida Indians did.

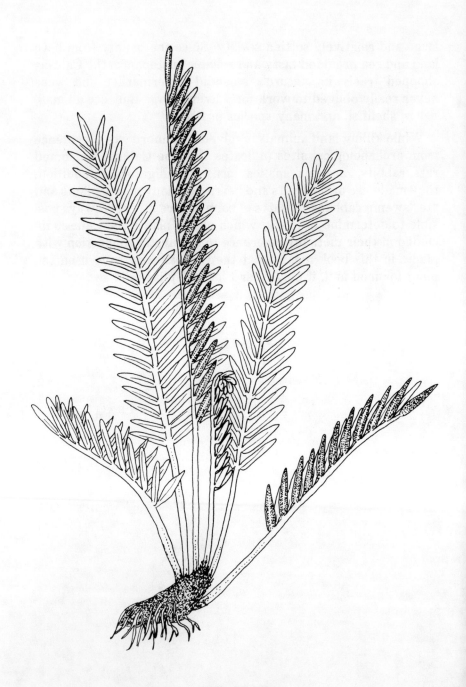

LEATHER FERN

LEATHER FERN
Acrostichum danaeaefolium

It is indeed hard to believe that the huge green fronds on the left side of the ramp belong to a fern. After all, ferns are supposed to look delicate and feathery; otherwise, florists would certainly not use them so much in their expensive flower arrangements. And yet, the fronds of the Leather Fern, the largest native fern in the United States, may be 12' long! Frankly, the Leather Fern looks like a monstrous, prehistoric plant that, by some freak of Nature, managed to escape extinction.

In fact, however, the Leather Fern is a dwarf when compared to the towering forests of ferns that flourished on this planet many millions of years ago. Indeed, ferns were so abundant during the Carboniferous Period that their remains contributed to the formation of coal. Prehistoric animals also tended to come in jumbo sizes, for big was definitely better during a period when it was far safer to be awesome and overwhelming. Although dinosaurs and other monsters of the earth were unable to adapt to drastic changes in the environment, ferns survived by becoming much smaller. Thus so far as survival of the fittest is concerned, the fittest are not necessarily the biggest.

Today, modest descendants of the giant, spore-bearing ferns live in the shadow of those parvenus, the seed-bearing plants. Since the Leather Fern is such an exceptionally large species, however, it serves to remind us that ferns once dominated the land many eons ago. Its common name is derived from the fact that the brown mass of spore cases on the underside of the leaflets feels like suede. The "fiddleheads," young fronds that resemble the head of a fiddle or violin, are edible when cooked like asparagus and the Indians took advantage of this free source of food.

WILD OLIVE
Forestiera segregata

Just beyond the Leather Fern, but on the right side of the ramp, are some Wild Olive shrubs. Like Wax Myrtle and Myrsine, Wild Olive grows all over Sanibel and often attains a height that is not normally associated with bushes. The mature fruit, about 1/2″ long, is very dark in color and does indeed contain a single stone or pit. Although a decent martini would require quite a number of such miniature olives, the bartender might find it difficult to beat the birds to Nature's minuscule bonanza.

The Wild Olive also produces tiny flowers, insignificant so far as we humans are concerned but quite worthy in the insect eyes of bees, mosquitoes and butterflies. Moreover, since the bark is rather rough, one often sees a variety of air plants perched on the branches of this shrub.

WILD COFFEE
Psychotria undata

The Wild Coffee on the left, opposite the Wild Olive, is yet another shrub that grows all over Sanibel. However, unlike the shrubs previously discussed, Wild Coffee never attempts to compete with trees in terms of height. Rather, it seems quite content to impress anyone who cares to look with the bright red berries that provide such a colorful contrast to its dark and very glossy green leaves. Indeed, the leaves are not only shiny but so distinctly veined as to appear quilted.

Wild Coffee does not have a monopoly on shiny leaves. Many other native species have rather glossy leaves that help protect them from the intense heat of the sun, thereby enabling them to retain precious moisture and survive in a subtropical climate. Wild Coffee's colorful red berries contain two tiny beans and, if one took the trouble to collect quite a number of them, one could indeed make a cup of coffee. However, botanists are sharply divided as to the merits of the brew.

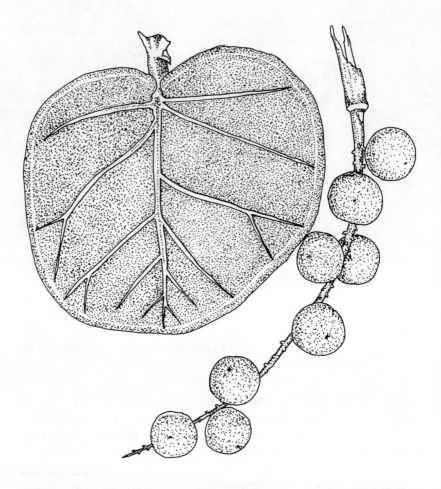

SEA GRAPE
Coccoloba uvifera

A curve now leads one to the top of the ramp and to a Sea Grape tree on the left which, like a number of the plants discussed so far, is invariably part of the dense mass of greenery in undeveloped areas. However, it is such a popular native tree that it is frequently planted around Sanibel's resorts and private homes. Wonderfully salt tolerant, the Sea Grape can thrive very near our Gulf beaches, attain a height of some 45′, and provide welcome shade from the intense rays of the sun.

Like so many native specimens, the Sea Grape does not lose all of its leaves at a particular time and expose its nudity to the world. Thus mature leaves, almost round and a good 8" wide, are constantly falling to the ground where, if Nature were allowed to take her course, they would decay and enrich our poor soil. Quite understandably, however, homeowners and resort managers take an exceedingly dim view of such litter, with the result that those who plant a Sea Grape tree must also buy a rake.

Up until a few years ago, visitors delighted in using Sea Grape leaves as post cards, and were quite willing to pay the letter rate in order to send cheerful messages to less fortunate friends and relatives who remained stranded in chilly climes. Alas, mechanization spelled the end of the Sea Grape post card.

In the introduction to this section, I indicated that the Sea Grape bears no grapes. Its common name is derived from the fact that the tree produces grape-like clusters of fruits that are about 3/4" long, pleasingly plump, and reddish purple upon maturity. Unlike grapes, however, individual members of the clusters do not ripen at the same time, their pits far outweigh the edible portion of the fruit, and no reputable vintner would ever claim that their flavor bore the slightest resemblance to that of real grapes.

It is indeed a fact that many people derive a great deal of pleasure and a real feeling of accomplishment from long hours of hard work, especially when the labor is purely voluntary and the results are either edible or potable. Thus in the fall, some Islanders make jelly and wine from the fruits of the Sea Grape.

One begins by spreading a sheet under a promising tree and shaking its branches quite vigorously so that the ripe fruits fall onto the sheet rather than onto the buggy ground. Subsequently, the large pits must be removed in order to obtain a paltry amount of pulp for making jelly or wine. Since it takes nine pounds of fruit to make eight, 6-ounce jars of jelly, the work involved must be a true labor of love. Sea Grape jelly is quite tasty, and the wine certainly has an overwhelming amount of "character."

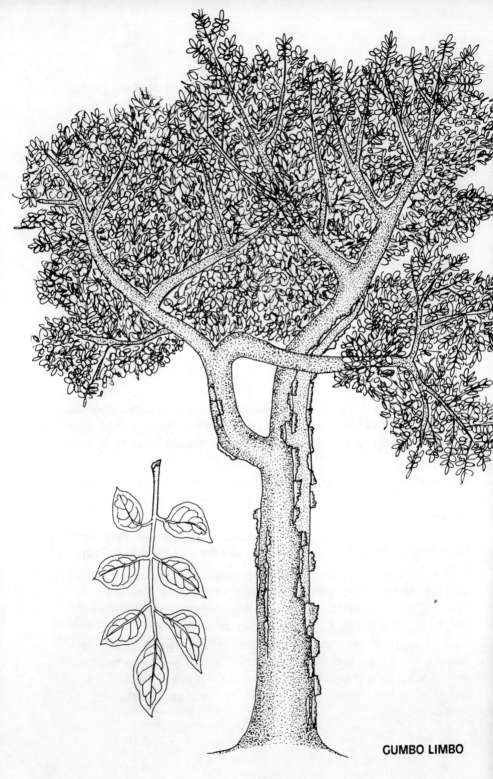

GUMBO LIMBO

GUMBO LIMBO
Bursera simaruba

Gumbo Limbo is certainly a very strange name for the native tree next to the Sea Grape! The name is apparently of African origin, derived from the Bantu, and that is about all the clarification that anyone can provide at the present time. This particular specimen is fairly young; older trees may reach a height of 60' and their trunks may be more than two feet in diameter.

Unlike the vast majority of Sanibel's native species, the Gumbo Limbo usually sheds most of its leaves in the fall. However, the temporary loss of leaves provides no impediment to identifying a tree that is instantly recognized by its outer bark. Smooth and wafer thin, extremely fine layers of the copper-tone bark are constantly peeling and curling. May the peeling propensities of this tree remind everyone, including Islanders who are often as pale as vanilla yogurt, that the sun's lethal rays make no distinction between visitors and residents!

Several centuries ago, the Indians tapped the Gumbo Limbo in order to obtain a heavy sap for sealing their canoes. Perhaps a clumsy brave cut himself in the process, with the result that the sap was found to be helpful in terms of coagulating the blood of minor wounds. Today, a major pharmaceutical company sells a concoction made from the Gumbo Limbo's sap for the treatment of gout.

One can cut a small branch off any Gumbo Limbo, stick it in the ground without much more ado, and it will quickly take root. Farmers have often used such branches to make "living fences" that are both practical and attractive. Since the wood is quite soft and easy to carve, many delighted children rode on the backs of carousel horses made from the Gumbo Limbo, until such splendid steeds were replaced by plastic or metal creations.

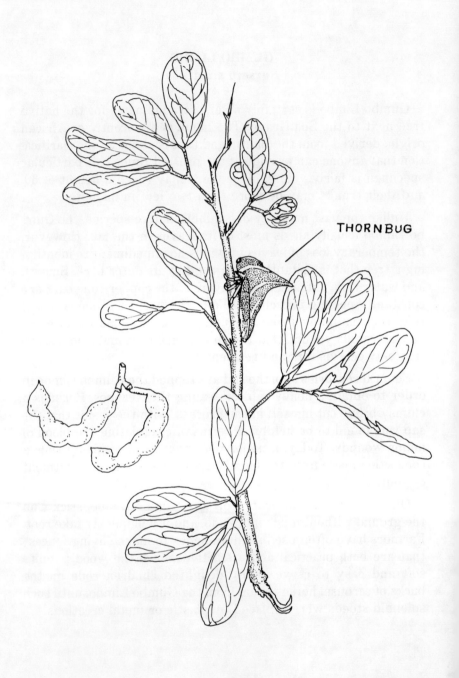

THORNBUG

CAT'S CLAW

CAT'S CLAW
Pithecellobium unguis-cati

The thorny native shrub in the corner is perfect for those gardeners who love planting but loathe pruning. While the Cat's Claw is not a self-pruning shrub, it attracts certain insects that do a fine job at no charge. A particular butterfly, the Miami Blue, likes to lay its eggs on Cat's Claw branches where their young larvae feast on new foliage. Although Thornbugs would certainly prefer to maintain a very low profile, you can easily find them all over the shrub's branches. When in doubt, give what appears to be a thorn a poke. If it moves, it's a Thornbug; if it doesn't, you may want to dab a bit of iodine on your finger.

Thornbugs belong to an order of insects (*Homoptera*) that are equipped with sucking mouthparts. Thus they are able to suck the juices from Cat's Claw branches. While sipping merrily on the branches, however, Thornbugs present an irresistible temptation to cardinals. In an effort to avoid becoming a delectable tidbit for birds, Thornbugs resort to deception or, more scientifically, "protective mimicry." The younger insects are green, the color of new thorns, while the adults adopt the darker color of older thorns. Although such chameleonic antics may initially confuse cardinals, the birds are generally patient enough to poke around and find a tasty treat.

While insects that live off the Cat's Claw may be of greater interest than the shrub itself, the thorns or spines that give this species its common name may be of considerable interest to those who heartily agree with Robert Frost's observation that "good fences make good neighbors." Certainly anyone who attempted to waltz through a hedge of Cat's Claw would soon have second thoughts upon surveying his torn clothes and scratched skin.

Having encountered nine of the most common species of native flora, visitors may wish to spend some time in the Center before going out on the trails. The Center houses a number of interesting exhibits featuring the island's ecology and vital wetlands, several of Sanibel's wild animals and birds and, of course, many of our famous shells.

OPOSSUM WITH YOUNG

CHAPTER 5.

MORE ALONG THE NATURE TRAILS

The Conservation Foundation maintains ten trails on its main tract, and it would take over four hours to walk them all! During the season, volunteer trail guides conduct several, one-hour tours nearly every day, and visitors are always welcome to explore the nature trails on their own throughout the year. For 50 cents, one can purchase a small booklet that identifies and describes over 30 numbered specimens along the Elisha Camp Trail, which takes about half an hour to cover at a comfortable pace.

Before going out on the trails, those who stop for a drink may notice a number of air plants perched along the wall above the water cooler. Extremely modest in appearance, it comes as quite a surprise to learn that such plants comprise about ten percent of the world's flowering species! Moreover, scientists are now finding them to be of considerable value in terms of monitoring air pollution. Although air plants are not identified on the Elisha Camp Trail, you will surely see them clinging to the branches of trees and shrubs that have rather rough bark. In any event, air plants certainly merit more than a footnote.

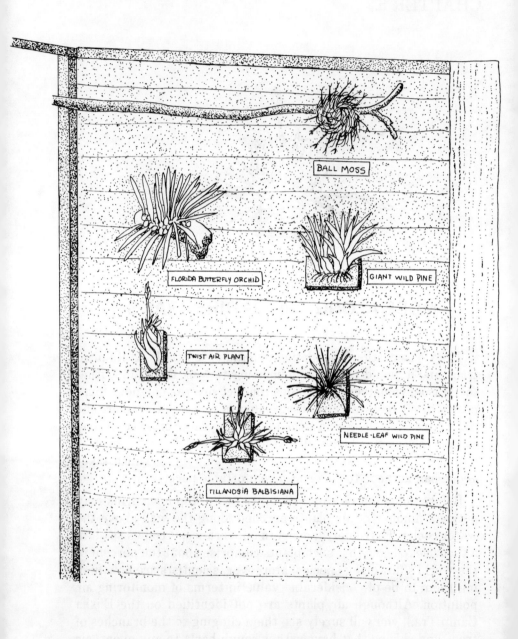

BALL MOSS

FLORIDA BUTTERFLY ORCHID

GIANT WILD PINE

TWIST AIR PLANT

NEEDLE-LEAF WILD PINE

TILLANDSIA BALBISIANA

AIR PLANTS

AIR PLANTS

Despite the fact that air plants always perch on other species or, as in the case of Spanish Moss, drape themselves rather languorously over branches, they never live off the hospitality of their hosts and are thus not parasites. Rather, some 30,000 species throughout the world are called "epiphytes," a heady scientific term denoting plants that derive much of their nourishment from rainfall which, as it drips through the forest canopy, picks up a number of minerals en route to the plants perched below.

Epiphytes are divided into two major groups: orchids and bromeliads. Of the two, the orchids (represented by the Florida Butterfly Orchid above the Center's water fountain), have always received devoted attention from horticulturists. After all, their blooms are both beautiful and, for once, not the least bit inconspicuous!

Scientists, on the other hand, have recently become far more fascinated by the bromeliads, an interest that has nothing to do with the fact that the latter are related to pineapples. Rather, it appears that those less flamboyant epiphytes (represented by six of the specimens above the water fountain), are such consummate scavengers that they pick up and store minute quantities of pollutants as well as vital minerals from the atmosphere in which they live. Scientists at Florida's Everglades National Park are currently monitoring bromeliads to determine whether emissions from the nuclear generators of the Florida Power and Light Company are polluting the air.

SPANISH MOSS

SPANISH MOSS
Tillandsia usneoides

Of all the air plants on display at the Center, Spanish Moss is probably the most familiar. Many people think that it looks rather weird, an eminently suitable cobweb for a house designed by Charles Addams as an ancestral home for the descendants of Frankenstein or Medusa. However, Calusa Indian women used to make a form of mini-skirt from Spanish Moss. Although the garment may have covered the bare essentials, it must have attracted bugs and itched dreadfully.

Tillandsia, the first part of this plant's scientific name (and that of all the other bromeliads thriving along the Center's wall), actually means nothing at all in Latin. Indeed, many species (*Virginia* this, *Eugenia* or *Blechnum* that) were named after various individuals for reasons that, more often than not, were best known to Sweden's famous 18th century botanist, Carl von Linné, better known as Linnaeus.

According to an old story that may well be apocryphal, Linnaeus believed that certain bromeliads did not like too much water. Therefore, he named them *Tillandsia* in honor of his good friend Dr. Tillands, thereby immortalizing the latter's frequent bouts of seasickness.

Affectionately referred to as "the little botanist" at the tender age of eight, his playmates may well have considered Linnaeus to be quite insufferable, just as later generations found Little Lord Fauntleroy to be utterly obnoxious. Be that as it may, the system for classifying plants and animals throughout the world is named after Linnaeus, a truly remarkable man who undertook the Herculean task of classifying all three of Nature's kingdoms.

BARN OWL

In leaving the Center to explore the nature trails, a small sign urges people to close the door quietly in order not to disturb Barn Owls that may be nesting in the wooden box affixed to one side of the building. Since development invariably destroys some of the natural habitats of wildlife, or renders their nesting areas unsafe, the Foundation has undertaken several projects designed to provide secure nesting sites for Ospreys, Black Skimmers and, in this instance, Barn Owls.

Although the staff did not know for a fact that any Barn Owls remained on these islands, they set up nesting boxes in suitable surroundings at several locations. It was not long before the Barn Owls gave proof of their existence and, most appropriately, the first box to be occupied was the one at the SCCF.

Since Barn Owls are Nature's peerless rat traps, their residence at the Center recently established the fact that the Rice Rat is not extinct on Sanibel, as had been feared. To be sure, the particular Rice Rat whose few identifiable remains proved that point is quite extinct.

WETLAND RIDGES AND SWALES

The trail begins at the boardwalk, which spans a swale that usually contains quite a bit of water. During the dry season, of course, there is far less water and much more mud. As indicated in Chapter 2, a fresh-water basin lies between the two main ridges that run roughly parallel to the Gulf and Bay shorelines. This particular swale is but a small part of over 1,000 acres of wetlands that represent relatively calm periods in the formation of the island.

Sanibel's interior wetlands do not form a single, continuous basin. Rather, the island's fresh-water system is composed of a number of swales separated by a series of very low ridges. Those ridges, generally measured in inches rather than in feet, bear silent testimony to stormy periods in Sanibel's development. A long time ago, such a ridge *was* the Gulf beach! Today, the ancient ridges of the wetlands provide a hospitable home for a great variety of flora and fauna.

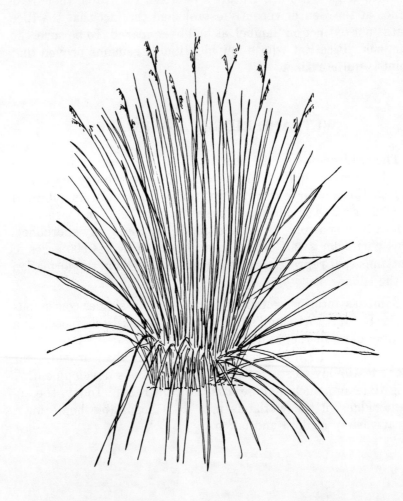

CORD GRASS

CORD GRASS
Spartina bakerii

Cord Grass is called an "indicator species" for its presence is a sure sign that one has come upon a swale. Since the plant requires what botanists refer to as "wet feet" for most of the year, clumps of Cord Grass thrive in our swales, often growing 6' high.

Like stalks of corn, to which this specimen is distantly related, its stems are sheathed by leaves. The roots of Cord Grass are quite unusual in that they are equipped with special membranes that prevent the invasion of salt into the plant's system. To the best of my knowledge, the red Mangrove is the only other species on Sanibel whose roots share this remarkable characteristic.

One might well wonder why the indicator species of *fresh*water wetlands should be equipped to resist the intrusion of *salt* water. The explanation for that seeming incongruity lies in the fact that the water in the wetlands is really more brackish than fresh, for there is always a certain amount of salt in the air on a barrier island. Moreover, since rainfall is rather negligible during the dry season, the salinity in the wetlands is quite high at that time.

Every year, the old grass on this plant dies off, thereby enriching the soil considerably. In fact, Cord Grass is so rich in minerals that its northeastern relative, known as Salt Marsh Hay, is actually harvested and sold to florists in order to provide nourishment for their plants. Although Sanibel's Cord Grass is too coarse for such commercial purposes, it serves a very important function by providing a home for many animals, as well as a happy hunting ground for their predators!

CABBAGE PALM
Sabal palmetto

Having crossed the swale, one comes upon a group of Cabbage Palms at the end of the boardwalk. One of eleven native species, the Cabbage Palm claims the distinction of being Florida's state tree, quite a singular honor in view of the fact that palms are really more closely related to grasses than to most trees! However, since the Cabbage Palm has helped Man in so many ways and continues to support a variety of flora and fauna, the considerable botanical difference between grasses and trees pales when compared to the services rendered by the Cabbage Palm.

The Cabbage Palm's berries are highly nutritious, although botanical opinion is sharply divided as to the merits of their flavor. In any event, those berries were a staple in the diet of local Indians who, in an effort to satisfy their stomachs and please their palates simultaneously, mixed them with water and herbs.

The Calusa Indians also ate the palm's large terminal buds, a South American variety of which is now canned and called "hearts of palm." Although Florida's Cabbage Palms can brave winds, storms and fires, they never survive the loss of their terminal buds. Alas, the nearby town of LaBelle hosts an annual "Swamp Cabbage Festival" that results in the mindless slaughter of some 1,500 palms in order to provide a few fleeting moments of palatable pleasure.

Our ancestors used the Cabbage Palm in a variety of ways. They made fans from the fronds (for flailing away at mosquitoes), built cabins and wharves from the trunks, extracted tannin from the roots, and medicine from the fruits. Apart from the annual outrage perpetrated upon Cabbage Palms at LaBelle, however, Florida's state tree now leads a peaceful life, lending welcome support to a considerable number of plants and wildlife.

Birds and raccoons feast on the berries with great gusto, giving nary a thought to their palatability, while lizards and various insects enjoy the moisture around the bud. One insect, the common cockroach, may have derived its euphemistic name (Palmetto Bug) from the fact that it is particularly partial to the dark, moist areas of old frond stems or "boots," the same areas in which the Strangler Fig tree often begins its life. Finally, the Cabbage Palm is frequently a living trellis for two vines, both of which are growing on the palms located at the end of the boardwalk.

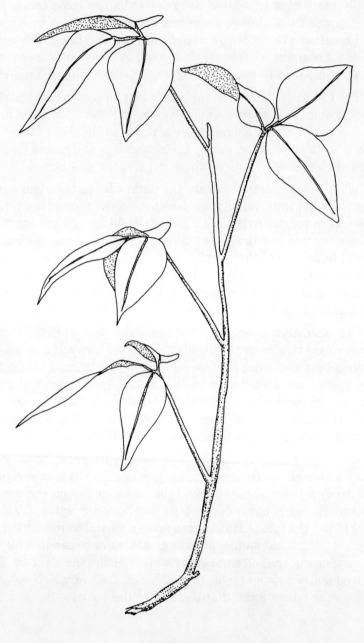

POISON IVY

POISON IVY
Toxicodendlon radicans

Of the two vines referred to at the end of the preceding paragraph, Poison Ivy deserves the immediate attention of anyone who is not already familiar with it. A twining vine with many groups of three, shiny green leaves, it should be avoided like the plague as you walk the trails. Poison Ivy may lurk close to the ground, reach out from the branches of harmless shrubs or, in a last-gasp effort, attempt to deceive you with the fiery red color of its dying leaves. Be it in the full bloom of youth or in flaming senility, the mere act of brushing against Poison Ivy causes many people to break out in a horrid rash, scratch incessantly, and spread the misery to other parts of their bodies.

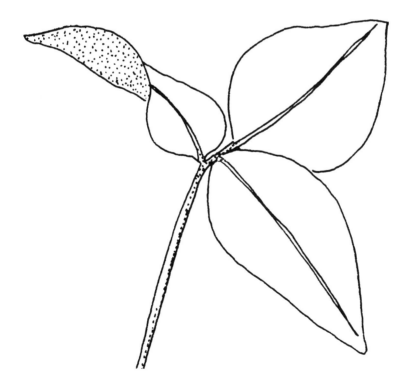

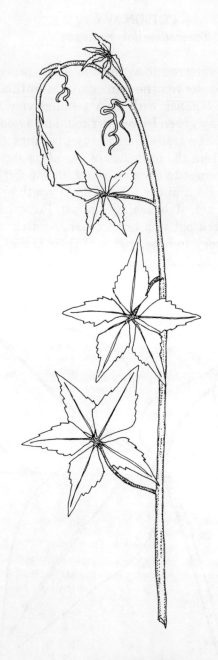

VIRGINIA CREEPER

VIRGINIA CREEPER (WOODBINE)
Parthenocissus quinquefolia

Like Poison Ivy, Virginia Creeper is a climbing vine that may grow as tall as the tree that serves as its trellis. Moreover, its leaves are green, and they also turn a brilliant scarlet color before dying. Indeed, the two vines are frequently found entwined on the same host! Therefore, count before you touch! Virginia Creeper has groups of five leaflets, whereas Poison Ivy has groups of three.

Virginia Creeper does produce small greenish flowers, inconspicuous to be sure, and blue-black berries follow the flowers. The Indians used to grind up the berries with the leaves and stalks in making a brew that served to settle their stomachs. The vine was introduced to Europe in the early 17th century and, when the Black Death (bubonic plague) broke out with a vengeance in England in the mid-1660s, a tea made from Virginia Creeper helped to reduce the fever of the plague's victims. Unfortunately, the brew never cured patients; it just made them more comfortable before sloughing off this mortal coil.

In later years, yet another concoction made from Virginia Creeper was sold as a hangover remedy in this country. However, it now appears that the vine's berries may be fatal to those who eat great quantities of them. Frankly, I cannot imagine why anyone would want to consume quantities of Virginia Creeper berries. However, it is perhaps wise to practice moderation in all things, lest one man's cure be another man's poison.

A STRANGE GROVE OF PALMS

Having reached the end of the boardwalk, a right turn onto the Elisha Camp Trail will soon lead one to the main Center Road. After walking just a few yards, you will see a small clearing on the left, bordered by familiar native plants: Wax Myrtle, Leather Fern and Myrsine. Of even greater interest, however, is the elliptical hole near the back of the clearing that is the home of quite a sociable creature, the Gopher Tortoise. More often than not, the reptile is in residence. (See Chapter 14.)

Just beyond the clearing, the trail winds through a refreshingly cool grove of Cabbage Palms where many Wild Coffee shrubs and various ferns seem to thrive in the shade. Virginia Creeper and Poison Ivy, of course, are crawling up the trunks of several mature trees, and have also extended their harmless invasion to very young palms that are no taller than a ten-year-old child. However, there is something rather strange about this grove, and a number of others that one encounters on the trails. The "boots" of older palms have burned off, leaving the trunks bare and black.

In 1973, lightning struck this property and the subsequent inferno consumed a vast amount of vegetation before it was finally brought under control. Only the Cabbage Palms survived, since the vital juices of palms are in the trunk while those of most trees are in the bark. The destruction of the outer bark is of little consequence to palms, but absolutely fatal to trees.

SANIBEL'S HOMESTEADERS
(c. 1880 - 1926)

Shortly after passing through the grove of charred Cabbage Palms leading charmed lives, one arrives at Center Road. At this juncture, a left turn onto that dirt road will lead one to the Observation Tower. However, those who make a very brief detour to the Booth Courtenay Trail directly across the road will be well rewarded with both a bit of island history and the sight of Sanibel's most colorful native tree.

At the very beginning of the Booth Courtenay Trail, a small clearing lies immediately to the left. While stumbling over several unexpected bumps in that grassy area may be rather annoying, the experience provides a fascinating glimpse into the past. Those small bumps and depressions are far too regular to represent turbulent and calm years in the formation of the island. Rather, they are the furrows of farmers, silent testimony to the presence of hardy homesteaders on Sanibel for some 40 years.

It is difficult to imagine that there was ever a time within living memory when Sanibel was not a full-fledged resort, a popular winter watering hole for thousands of visitors. In fact, however, this barrier island was quite isolated from the mainland until 1963, when the completion of the Causeway resulted in the demise of the ferry and, inevitably, the end of an era. While many mourn those halcyon days of B.C. (Before Causeway), Sanibel's homesteaders certainly found the island of yore to be less than idyllic!

The farming community braved billions of mosquitoes and survived several hurricanes in order to make a modest profit from growing eggplants, tomatoes, peppers, watermelons and grapefruit. In September of 1926, however, an especially severe hurricane brought an abrupt end to commercial farming on Sanibel. Its 14-foot tides sowed salt throughout the island, a legacy that would take years to leach out.

One is often told that the hurricane of 1926 ruined farming forever. And yet, the salt has obviously leached out sufficiently since so many Islanders are justly proud of their vegetable gardens. However, it is certainly safe to say that the land is now totally unsuitable for commercial farming, since no one in his right mind would pay a king's ransom for resort property in order to plant peppers!

Not all Islanders abandoned Sanibel by the end of 1926. Some remained to meet the needs of fishermen, shellers, nature lovers, and several colonies of devoted "Snowbirds" who migrated every winter to simple, Gulf-front cottages. However, one particular link between the past and the present has survived all vicissitudes.

Just before arriving on Sanibel, those who look to the right can still see the pilings of the wharf from which the farmers' produce was shipped, and the small white building of the exporting firm that also served as a general store. The Sanibel Packing Company is still very much alive and well. It moved to a better location many years ago, and nearly every visitor soon becomes familiar with the peerless emporium that is now called Bailey's General Store.

CHEROKEE BEAN (CORAL BEAN)
Erythrina herbacea
(see color section)

Quite understandably, not everyone is enthralled by the furrows of former farmers. However, the clearing also contains a splendid specimen of what may well be the most colorful and toxic native tree on Sanibel. Over 20′ tall at maturity, the Cherokee Bean is easily identified by the distinctive, arrowhead shape of its green leaves. In late winter and throughout the spring, when the leaves are not present, no one could fail to recognize the flaming blooms that resemble short, scarlet spikes.

Since this plant belongs to the pea family, it dutifully produces black pods which, in the fall, burst open and scatter red-orange beans upon the ground. Indians liked the bright beans so much that they frequently used them to make colorful necklaces. Moreover, since they were constantly concocting brews out of beans and berries, the Indians found that an arrowhead dipped in Cherokee Bean brew would kill small game.

Although it can never be proved, it is quite conceivable that the fatal Calusa arrow that lodged in Ponce de Leon's leg *may* have been coated with that toxic brew. While the Indians also experimented with Cherokee Bean tea, they soon gave up the practice when they found that a very small dose caused them to hallucinate, and a larger amount could kill them.

The Cherokee Bean is by far my favorite tree. Unlike most native species, it provides a highly colorful contrast to the dense mass of green as one drives along the Sanibel-Captiva Road. There is a nice specimen in the public park on Periwinkle, and a fine young Cherokee Bean greets visitors as they approach the "Ding" Darling Center. While many of Sanibel's introduced species rival the Cherokee Bean in terms of beauty, none can hold a candle to that native's ability to survive!

As is the case with the Gumbo Limbo, one can take a cutting from a Cherokee Bean, plant it in the ground, and subsequently be rewarded for one's benign neglect by the growth of a new tree. However, when a friend and I were determined to save a lovely Cherokee Bean from death by development, the hapless tree was constantly plagued by malign intervention and rarely enjoyed a moment of benign neglect!

The tree was literally hacked out of the ground when in full bloom, its roots savaged by a sharp shovel. It was then dragged through the woods and dumped unceremoniously into the trunk of a car. Although the ravaged roots rested in the trunk, the trailing branches and blooms were severely scraped by the hard surface of the road during the three-mile drive to the site of the plant's supposed salvation. The battered Cherokee Bean was finally planted by a lake in the inhospitable "soil" composed of sand and shells, and christened with a bucketful of Sanibel water.

Shortly thereafter, the tree was mercilessly pruned, its wounds slopped with ugly black goo, and only then was it left to its own devices. It produced new growth within two weeks, and then dozens of those distinctive, arrowhead leaves appeared. Alas, some men came to trim nearby trees and, in the process, guillotined the Cherokee Bean! And yet, that tree is thriving today, *despite* our efforts to save it. Moreover, several of its ill-fated limbs will eventually become fine trees in their own right, including one that was left lying on the ground for ten days in defiance of death.

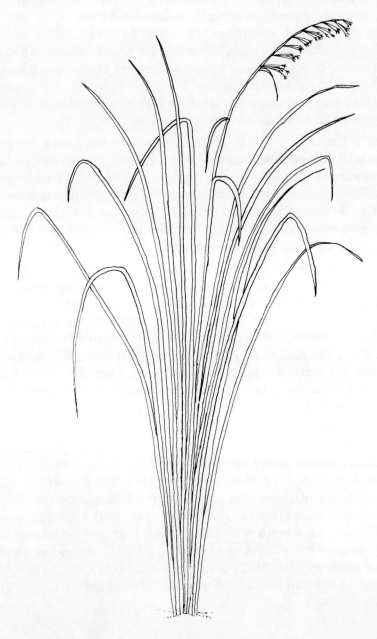

SAW GRASS

SAW GRASS
Cladium jamaicensis

No one who walks the trails will want to miss a splendid view of the Sanibel River, a close look at an Osprey nest, the sight of a red-beaked Gallinule behaving like a duck, or an introduction to a very common plant with the potential to feed the world. Thus it is time to return to Center Road, turn right, and walk to the Observation Tower.

Along the way, one sees masses of Cord Grass and Leather Fern, lovers of "wet feet" whose presence clearly indicates a swale region. Moreover, Saw Grass is very much in evidence for it, too, is particularly partial to marshy areas. Those who visit Sanibel in the late spring and early summer will enjoy the sight of dense tufts of dark, red-brown seed heads swaying gracefully in the breeze.

Despite its common name, Saw Grass is really a sedge and not a grass, a distinction that is difficult to grasp since sedges are so often referred to as being grasslike. Unlike grasses, however, sedges usually have solid triangular stems, three rows of pointed leaves with vicious sawlike teeth, and tiny blooms. Surely anyone who attempted to charge through a clump of Saw Grass would end up with torn clothing and multiple lacerations!

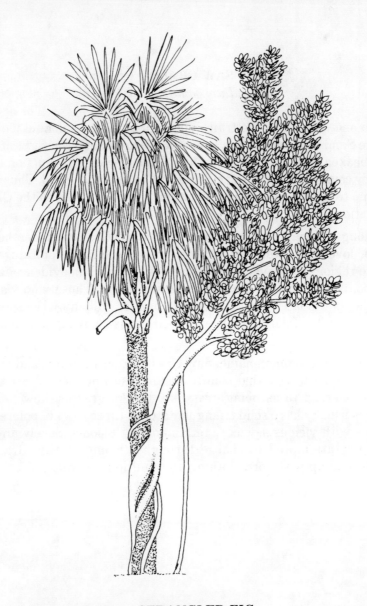

STRANGLER FIG
Ficus aurea

Center Road ends in a clearing and one can see the Observation Tower just ahead. At this point, many people like to pause for a moment and enjoy the view from a bend in the Sanibel River. Those who are weary from walking will be delighted by the presence of benches! Whether sitting or standing, one is immediately aware of two entirely different trees standing side by side, silent sentinels of that particular bend in the river. The one with peeling, reddish bark is, of course, a Gumbo Limbo. The other is commonly known by a most unflattering name, Strangler Fig.

The tallest *native* tree on Sanibel, the Strangler Fig may germinate from a seed dropped on the ground, probably by a bird, and eventually grow some 60′ tall. Given its height and dense masses of leaves, the Strangler Fig is a splendid shade tree that provides no clue as to the origin of its nasty name. However, the species does not always grow in the traditional manner of trees. More often than not, it begins life many feet *above* the ground!

Birds are clearly responsible for the fact that the Strangler Fig frequently starts out as an epiphyte, for the tree produces sweet golden fruits (just over half an inch long) that the former find utterly delectable. Having gorged upon the fruits, birds subsequently drop the undigested seeds on the ground or in the nooks and crannies of trees.

Although the Cabbage Palm is by no means the sole beneficiary of the jettisoned bounty of birds, its fronds and "boots" provide an especially hospitable home for such bird byproducts. Thus in no time at all, a seed sprouts and sends roots to the ground. Some make their way down by wrapping themselves around the trunk of the host, while others descend from the host's branches like the aerial roots of a Banyan tree and bear a strong resemblance to guy wires.

Despite the Strangler Fig's propensity to wrap itself around other trees, especially the Cabbage Palm, it is not the boa constrictor of the plant world. It may live in epiphytic harmony with its host for many years without strangling the latter in a deadly embrace. Should the host die, a coroner would probably attribute its demise to the lack of sufficient sunlight, and the Strangler Fig would have to plead guilty.

Anhinga

Marsh Rabbit

Tricolored Heron

Brown Pelican

65

White Ibis

Cattle Egret

Snowy Egret

Cherokee Bean

Royal Poinciana

Bougainvillea

Ixora

Hibiscus

67

Oleander

Florida River Otter

Sea Hibiscus

Periwinkle

68

Young opossum in Cabbage Palm

Young raccoon

Key West Anole

Gopher Tortoise

69

Double-Crested Cormorant

Little Blue Heron

Black Skimmer

Great Blue Heron

70

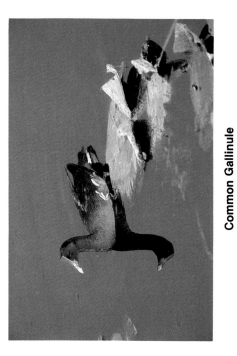

Common Gallinule

Feral Feline (Wild Cat)

Osprey

Great Egret

Roseate Spoonbill

Alligator

72

COMMON GALLINULE
(See photo in color section)

Unlike plants, birds are totally unreliable. A bird that perches on the limb of a particular tree one day will probably not pause in the same place the next day or, for that matter, the next minute. On the other hand, the reliable tree remains rooted to the same spot until it dies. Fortunately, the Gallinule is neither skittishly shy nor afflicted by wanderlust. Thus one can generally count on seeing a Common Gallinule at this bend in the river, as well as in the fresh waters of Sanibel's lakes and ponds.

Common Gallinules behave very much like ducks as they feed and swim in the water, frequently accompanied by the equally ducklike American Coots. However, the Gallinule's flaming red forehead and beak immediately distinguish it from its less flamboyant companions. In addition to swimming about and feeding, Gallinules love to tramp around Cattails, grasses, and reeds whose dead stems provide highly suitable nesting material. A female Gallinule may lay nearly a dozen eggs, and it is extremely gratifying for a female author and mother to note that the male takes turns with its mate throughout the boring incubating process.

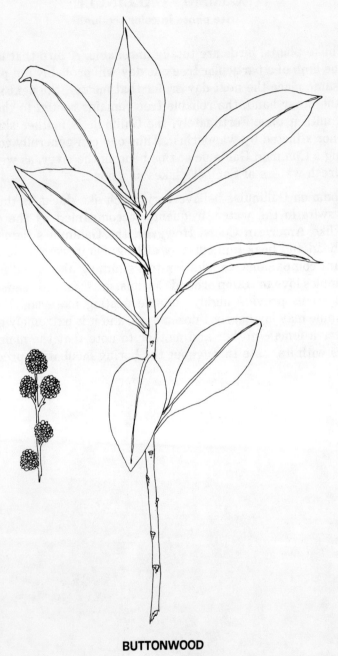

BUTTONWOOD

BUTTONWOOD (BUTTON MANGROVE)
Conocarpus erecta

Having rested on the benches at the clearing, or at least paused for a few moments, one is now ready for a short stroll to the Observation Tower. Just before crossing the footbridge, however, there is a tree on the left that certainly merits an introduction. Its common name comes from the tough fruits, less than 1″ in diameter, that bear a striking resemblance to tiny leather buttons.

The Indians were particularly partial to Buttonwood trees for their hard wood made a splendid fire with a minimum of smoke, a highly desirable attribute in the eyes of those who did not always wish to announce their presence to everyone in the vicinity. Subsequently, our ancestors found that the tree burned as well as high-grade charcoal, with the result that countless Buttonwoods were felled and sold at a handsome profit in order to feed the fires of seagoing ships. Thus it was not long before the Buttonwood became a threatened, if not an endangered, species.

Fortunately, modern ships do not burn Buttonwoods, and the trees are making a good comeback. Those who enjoy the adventure of a canoe trip on the Sanibel River will see scores of Buttonwoods, many of which are fine old specimens whose trunks were bent and contorted by severe storms. Such bowed but unbroken survivors are frequently festooned with air plants that are attracted by the comfortable perches and, of course, by the rough bark.

Visitors at the "Ding" Darling Refuge will certainly see a great many Buttonwoods along Wildlife Drive, and their presence on the bay side of this island explains why the tree is often called a Button Mangrove. Although the Buttonwood is really not a mangrove, it lives in very close association with three other trees that are also called mangroves — even though only one of them is truly a mangrove! In any event, all four "mangroves" are supremely salt tolerant, they help build up the land, and their many virtues will be discussed in the next chapter.

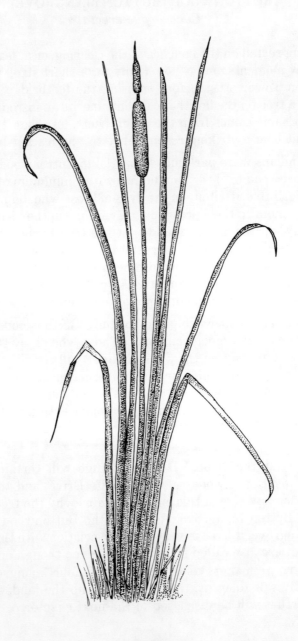

CATTAIL

CATTAIL(S)
Typha domingensis

In crossing the narrow wooden footbridge, it is easy to ignore the lowly Cattails on the left. After all, those ubiquitous plants thrive in shallow water, be it brackish or fresh, in many parts of our country. Thus their presence by the footbridge contributes nothing to the *je ne sais quoi* that one seeks on Sanibel. Indeed, most people are very familiar with the Cattail's crowning glory: two flower heads that bear some resemblance to hot dogs but absolutely none to the tail of a cat. In certain species, the flower heads are joined, whereas those of the Cattail that one most commonly sees on Sanibel are separated. Be they joined or separated, the male flower head always enjoys the better view from the top!

A Sanibel resident who grew up in rural Illinois in the 1920s recalls that Cattails made fine torches for those who wanted to go frogging, fishing, or dash to the outhouse at night. Once dipped in kerosene and ignited, the flower heads lighted the way — often enveloping the torchbearer in smudge. However, it now appears that the common Cattail offers much more than torches and nesting material for birds, with the result that several organizations actively encourage the cultivation of this plant in many parts of the world.

From top to bottom, this remarkable plant is both edible and nutritious. The young flower heads can be boiled and eaten like corn on the cob, and one can make flour from the pollen of mature flower heads. The young stalks and shoots may be peeled and added to salads or cooked like a vegetable, while on the roots one finds sprouts suitable for a salad, a cooked vegetable, a potato, or even a pickle! Although the food products derived from Cattails will probably never grace the gourmet sections of American supermarkets, Cattail salads, vegetables and flour may ensure human survival in less fortunate areas of the world.

AN OSPREY PLATFORM

On the other side of the wooden footbridge, a short trail leads to the Observation Tower. The path is lined with Leather Fern, Wax Myrtle, Salt Bush, and mounds of sand and shells deposited by the dredgers (not by the Calusa Indians). Buttonwoods grow by the banks of the peaceful river, birds call to one another, and a rather discordant noise in the background that sounds like "onk onk" may indicate the presence of either a bullfrog or an alligator. Those who cannot distinguish one "onk" from another may wish to climb to the very top of the Observation Tower without further ado.

The Observation Tower provides a fine view of the river, the surrounding area, and an Osprey nest that adorns a tall wooden platform. More often than not, the raptor is in residence and this splendid species will be discussed in a later chapter. At this point, however, it is interesting to know why the Conservation Foundation, together with a number of concerned individuals, felt that it was necessary to erect over 40 platforms on Sanibel and Captiva since there is clearly no shortage of the high nesting sites so favored by these birds.

Unfortunately, the Ospreys took a fancy to tall utility poles. During the rainy season, seepage from their nests often ate through the insulation on wires, thereby causing short circuits, "outages," and, occasionally, the electrocution of birds. One might well wonder how seepage from an Osprey nest could cause pandemonium at the local power company. After all, the bird builds its nest with fairly conventional materials: sticks lined with soft grasses, vines, *etc.* However, one has to consider what may be *inside* the nest of an avid junk collector.

Those who brave high ladders in order to peek into the premises report the following finds: a rag doll, a bath towel, a straw hat, a broom, bottles, cans, sea shells, shirts, *etc.*, *etc.* Moreover, Ospreys constantly add on to their homes and, since the same nest may be occupied for over 30 years, it grows like Topsy, becomes extraordinarily heavy, and looks utterly unkempt!

Thus the Osprey platforms scattered throughout the islands represent an effort to encourage the raptors to forsake utility poles in favor of safer and less disruptive nesting sites. The fact that well over half of those platforms are currently occupied is a fine tribute to Man's ingenuity, and to the Osprey's adaptability.

CHAPTER 6.

OTHER NOTABLE NATIVES

Although the extensive tract of land at the Conservation Center provides a fine introduction to native vegetation, not all indigenous species inhabit the interior wetlands. Thus while a few of the plants discussed in this chapter may grow in the wetlands, most are more commonly associated with other parts of the island. Fortunately, one need not travel very far to find them.

In a truly remarkable display of unanimity, both Islanders and developers agree that the aesthetic merits of some species (palms in particular) warrant their presence on the grounds of Sanibel's residences and resorts. Other natives, like lovely wildflowers and the lowly Dog Fennel, are both ubiquitous and utterly oblivious to Man's obsession with planned planting. However, the unsung heroes of Sanibel are those native species that guard the relatively peaceful shores of Pine Island Sound and San Carlos Bay or, anchored in the shifting sands along the Gulf of Mexico, brave full exposure to the elements.

GUARDIANS OF THE BEACH

All native vegetation on Sanibel is equipped to cope with salt to varying degrees. However, the pioneer plants that grow along our Gulf shores must be supremely salt tolerant in order to survive occasional flooding and constant exposure to saline spray. Furthermore, they must be endowed with a highly elaborate root system that can thrive in sandy "soil," withstand the ravages of storms and winds and, God willing, help hold the island together until the next tourist season.

Most of the beach grasses and creeping vines are of very little interest to the average beachcomber, until he howls in anguish when Sand Spurs lodge in the tender soles of his bare feet. But since beach vegetation performs a veritable labor of Hercules, no one really has a right to expect it to be a thing of beauty and a joy forever as well! However, one of the grasses is extremely attractive, frequently immortalized by writers and artists, and so effective in preventing erosion that it is fully protected under Florida law. That simple, indispensable grass is called Sea Oats.

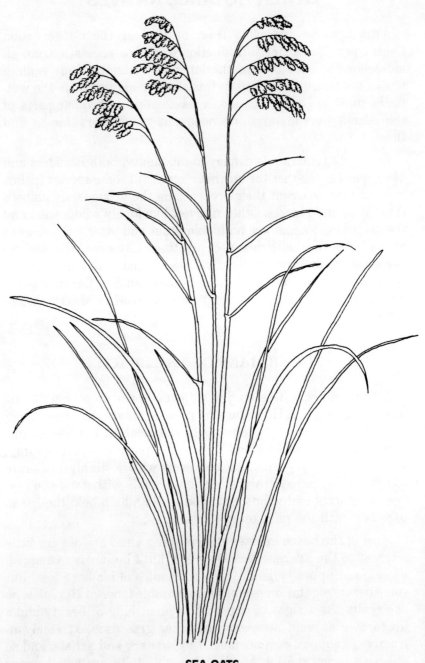

SEA OATS

Sea Oats
Uniola paniculata

While many species of beach vegetation form the island's first line of defense, grasses are the peerless pioneers at the point. In terms of stabilizing our Gulf beaches and preventing erosion, their presence is essential. Of all the grasses that grow along the Atlantic and Gulf coasts from Virginia to Texas, the perennial Sea Oats play such a vital role that they are deemed worthy of legal protection in the State of Florida. Thus it is against the law to pick Sea Oats anywhere in Florida.

Fortunately, Sea Oats are utterly undaunted by shifting sands. In fact, they seem to thrive in such a precarious environment and generally grow in rather dense clumps. Seed heads bearing a strong resemblance to oats grace the tops of their stems and, while it is illegal to harvest them in Florida, some species provide flour for residents in other parts of the world.

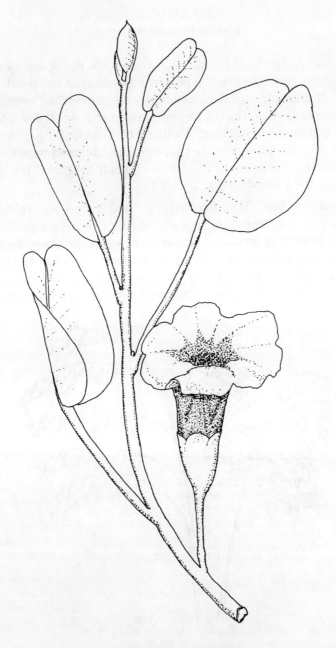

BEACH MORNING GLORY

Beach Morning Glory (Railroad Vine)
Ipomoea pes-caprae

Although beach plants are extraordinarily hardy, nothing ever grows *below* the normal tide line. After all, the waters of the Gulf reclaim the lower beach every day at high tide and, during stormy periods, that zone bears the full brunt of the destructive power of pounding waves. While the lower beach is certainly a sheller's paradise, it is no garden of Eden for plants!

Just *above* the tide line, however, several grasses and vines sink their extensive roots into the shifting sands and broken bits of shells. Beach Morning Glory, a vine that can creep and twine for well over 25 yards, is frequently one of the first to occupy and defend that highly hazardous zone. Like its equally brave comrades, the vine not only survives but actually thrives! Unlike the former, however, Beach Morning Glory is beautiful.

The lovely, purplish flowers, shaped like the speakers on old gramophones in the age of "His Master's Voice," account for the word 'glory' in the vine's common name. 'Morning' refers to the fact that the flowers always open in the morning and generally close by noon, for only mad dogs and Englishmen go out in the noonday sun.

The vine's leaves are quite large when compared to those of other beach plants and, not surprisingly, they are very green and glossy. Moreover, they are edible. Thus ardent shellers who become engrossed to the point of starvation can always sustain life until the tide rolls in and it is time to go home.

DOG FENNEL

THE EDIBLE FENNEL
Eupatorium capillifolium

As indicated at the beginning of this chapter, Dog Fennel is ubiquitous. Indeed, the perennial herb thrives within a few yards of our Gulf beaches, springs up along the sides of every island road (unless mowed), and is one of the first natives to reappear on cleared construction sites in brazen defiance of the best efforts of bulldozers. Since it is impossible to miss Dog Fennel on Sanibel, many people inquire about "that green thing that looks like wild asparagus."

While Dog Fennel may be less than a foot high early in the spring, it is often 6' tall by the end of the summer rainy season. The herb frequently grows in clumps, and every stem is covered with extraordinarily fine leaves. The plant's common name may be derived from the fact that its fluffy crown of leaves bears some resemblance to a dog's tail. However, I have never known a canine endowed with quite such a soft tail, and certainly not a green one.

Although the visible portion of Dog Fennel does indeed look something like wild asparagus, asparagus lovers would quickly point out that the former cannot hold a candle to the latter. However, Sanibel's lowly herb is edible and may be added to salads, gravies, sauces, or any other food that might benefit from the flavor of fennel.

Finally, I should mention that Dog Fennel once caused considerable consternation on this island. A few years ago, the wife of a visiting head of state received a special guided tour at the Conservation Center. The lady in question proved to be both remarkably knowledgeable about native flora and extraordinarily eager to sample our edible plants. However, she attacked Dog Fennel with such gusto that her security guards became visibly alarmed, with the result that the guides felt obliged to consume quantities of that herb without checking for the presence of bugs.

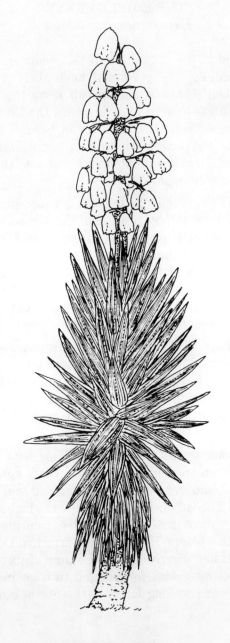

SPANISH BAYONET

SPANISH BAYONET
Yucca aloifolia

Like Dog Fennel, Spanish Bayonet grows all over Sanibel, albeit in less profusion. It peeps out from the dense foliage along Casa Ybel and Sanibel-Captiva Roads, decorates the public park on Periwinkle, and is frequently planted by Islanders at the borders of their lawns. Unlike Dog Fennel, however, the Spanish Bayonet is not a plant that one can bump into with impunity, unless one happens to be wearing a full suit of armor!

Spanish Bayonet is well named, for its stem is completely surrounded by a fierce array of stiff, sword-like leaves (about 1½' long) that are extremely sharp and unpleasantly pointed. As is so often the case, however, a threatening exterior is crowned with beautiful blooms. Thus in late spring and early summer, the Spanish Bayonet produces not just one waxy white flower but entire clusters of those bell-shaped beauties.

Everyone delights in the beautiful blooms of the Spanish Bayonet, including the Yucca moth that fertilizes the plant by laying its eggs in the flowers. Moreover, in addition to being very lovely, the flowers are edible. An imaginative hostess might add the creamy white petals to a salad or dip them in cocktail spreads, thereby enhancing her reputation by creating a culinary sensation.

Since the leaves and stems of the Spanish Bayonet are very tough and fibrous, characteristics shared by other members of the *Yucca* family, the Indians often used the fibers in making baskets, footwear, and evey pottery. Today, however, people are far more interested in the threatening exterior of the Spanish Bayonet, a definite deterrent to trespassers, and in the fact that this native plant is supremely salt tolerant, never requires any watering, or fertilizing, and thus makes no demands upon an Islander's time, energy or pocketbook.

THE PREHISTORIC PALMS

Palms invariably conjure up visions of unspoiled tropical isles, endless sandy beaches, and delightfully romantic interludes beneath their palmate or pinnate leaves. Since Florida's economy is so heavily dependent upon tourism, the Sunshine State is indeed fortunate to be blessed with eleven native species, more than any other state in the country. Thus the combination of tropical sun and palms gives Florida a distinct advantage in attracting those seeking both an escape and an earthly Eden without applying for a passport.

As indicated in the preceding chapter, palms are really closely related to grasses. However, that nit-picking observation in no way diminishes the ineffable image enjoyed by palms. Moreover, there are several thousand species of palms throughout the world, and fossil remains prove that palms existed in the Age of the Dinosaurs some 55 million years ago.

While ferns are considerably older than palms, perhaps 350 million years older by geological reckoning, there is nothing at all romantic about them and they are of little economic value. Ferns are certainly not a tourist attraction, and one must wait countless eons until their carbonized remains contribute to the formation of coal. Thus the economic importance of ferns is largely limited to their use in floral arrangements. However, the economic importance of the parvenu palms is considerable.

Although Florida's residents once used palms extensively, especially the Cabbage Palm, their commercial value is primarily limited to landscaping and local honey. In other parts of the world, however, palm products still play an important role in the economy. Such products include dates and coconuts, building material and fiber, wax and wine, and the stimulating betel nuts chewed by Bloody Mary in the famous Broadway show, *South Pacific*. Finally, it is estimated that the teeming population of India annually consumes 800 million pounds of palm sugar!

Of the eleven species of palms that are native to Florida, three are most commonly seen on Sanibel. Since the Cabbage Palm has already been discussed in Chapter 5, the following section will be devoted to the other two. While the Saw Palmetto may shatter one's image of stately palms, the Coconut Palm will certainly make amends for any temporary disillusionment.

Saw Palmetto
Serenoa repens

Although the Saw Palmetto may be the most abundant palm in Florida, it is probably not anyone's idea of a proper palm. Indeed, 10′ would be a rather dizzy height for a palm that is usually little more than a sprawling shrub. The Saw Palmetto derives its name from the fact that its stem is sharply toothed, like a saw. While the specimen bears a strong resemblance to a young Cabbage Palm, a close examination of the stem provides instant (and possibly painful) identification.

All palms are divided into two major categories, based upon the appearance of their leaves. Thus leaves arranged like a feather on both sides of a central midrib are called pinnate, as contrasted with palmate leaves that are fan shaped, like the palm of one's hand. The leaves of the Saw Palmetto are distinctly palmate and almost form a circle, about 3′ wide.

In terms of edibility, the Saw Palmetto has a great deal in common with the Cabbage Palm. It, too, produces small berries (about 1″ long) that were an important source of food for the Indians. Moreover, its terminal bud, although much smaller than that of the Cabbage Palm, is indeed edible. Needless to say, cutting it out will kill the plant. Finally, the Saw Palmetto's small white flowers are extremely fragrant, attract swarms of bees, and the final result of that attraction is called "Palmetto Honey" and is marketed commercially.

COCONUT PALM

Coconut Palm
Cocos nucifera

Unlike the rather scrubby Saw Palmetto, the Coconut Palm is certainly everyone's idea of a proper palm. It soars 80' into the air, invariably leans at a picturesque angle, and its 15-foot, pinnate leaves rustle in the breeze. Indeed, this is the romantic palm that natives scurried up and down in Hollywood movies of a bygone era.

As indicated in Chapter 1, a coconut shares the Red Mangrove seedling's ability to float in salt water for an extended period of time before landing and taking root in whatever passes for *terra firma* in a hospitable clime. Although some of the Coconut Palms on Sanibel did indeed arrive in this natural manner, the overwhelming majority crossed the Causeway in large trucks and became the instant, mature specimens that now grace our resorts.

Certainly there is nothing wrong with the practice of importing additional native vegetation to enhance the beauty of the island. Moreover, the fact that our resorts were built before their mature Coconut Palms were planted in no way diminishes one's pleasure in beholding such magnificent specimens. Of course, whenever a major storm or hurricane threatens to unleash its mighty winds and wrath, a resort manager must hire people to pull the coconuts out of all those palms lest such potential projectiles break every window in the place.

Everyone is well aware of the economic importance of coconuts: the "milk", the shredded interior, and the oil that is added to tanning products. During the season, many people like to mail coconuts to snowbound friends and relatives. The recipients are doubtless delighted by such a unique gift, if they can crack it open.

DEFENDERS OF THE BAY

The four species of pioneer trees that build up and protect the shores and inland areas along the bay are something of a botanical embarrassment because they are all called mangroves, but only one of them is a true mangrove. In fact, one does not need to understand a single word of Latin to realize that those trees belong to four different genera!

Moreover, their common names merely add to the confusion since anyone can see that the Red Mangrove is not visibly red, the Black and the White Mangroves do not display their assigned colors, and only the Button Mangrove discussed in Chapter 5 bears a common name that makes any sense at all. However, the four trees are such close neighbors and have so much in common that it may not be too outrageous to take certain liberties with scientific precision and continue the tradition of calling them mangroves.

Mangroves are literally the *sine qua non* in terms of building up and defending the land along San Carlos Bay and Pine Island Sound, thereby transforming a spit of sand into a barrier island. In this connection, there is a definite pecking order or "plant succession," which simply means that the first species in line builds up the land and provides a hospitable home for the second species, which in turn performs the same service for its successor, *etc.*

As indicated in Chapter 1, the Red Mangrove is the first and indispensable pioneer, the bravest of the brave, and the only true mangrove on this island. The Black Mangrove is not far behind, the White Mangrove is something of a laggard but certainly not a coward, and the Button Mangrove waits until its three predecessors have created suitable terrain before establishing itself.

In order to build up and defend the shoreline and inland regions, all mangroves must be exceptionally salt tolerant. Thus the roots of the Red Mangrove are equipped with special membranes that prevent salt from entering the tree's system, whereas the other mangroves expel salt from their leaves. Wildlife Drive in the "Ding" Darling Refuge offers the best opportunity to see the four pioneer mangroves that are so essential to both the creation and the continued existence of Sanibel Island.

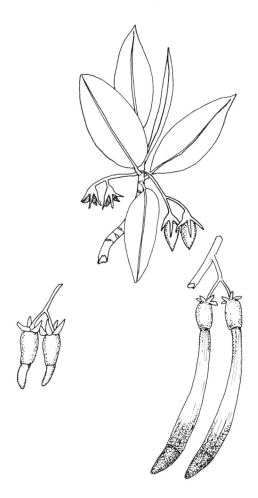

Red Mangrove
Rhizophora mangle

Since the Red Mangrove has already been discussed at considerable length in Chapter 1, readers are well aware of the fact that this tree is the premier pioneer on off-shore sand spits like Sanibel and Captiva. Once established, it becomes our first line of defense along the bay, provides a home and a hunting ground for a vast variety of wildlife, and produces a prodigious amount of food in the form of detritus for all manner of fish and shellfish. Thus the entire world, quite apart from tiny barrier islands such as ours, is deeply indebted to the extraordinary ability of an 8" seedling to survive and thrive against overwhelming odds.

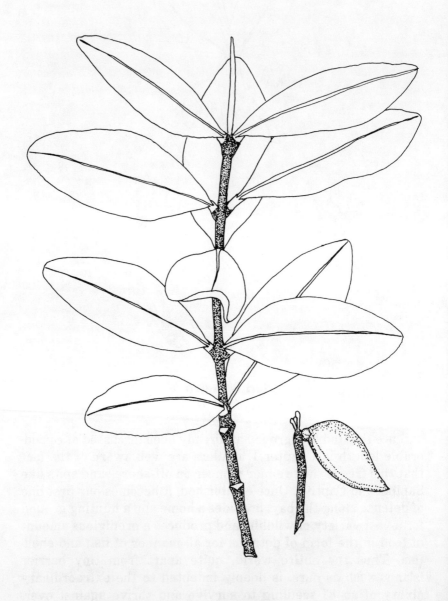

BLACK MANGROVE

Black Mangrove
Avicennia germinans

Although the distance that separates one kind of mangrove from another is often a matter of a few yards, the four species dominate entirely different zones, and each is specially equipped to cope with its particular environment. Thus the Red Mangrove reigns supreme along the swampy shoreline and, moving inland a bit, the Black Mangrove dominates the next zone and grows to a height of over 50′.

One might think that Black Mangroves enjoy a far more hospitable environment than Red Mangroves, since the latter grow along a mucky shoreline that is flooded every day at high tide. However, such is not at all the case. Although the Black Mangrove zone is inundated only during extremely high tides, it often remains flooded for quite a period of time, with the result that the soil has a very high salt content and the malodorous mud contains very little oxygen.

Fortunately, the Black Mangrove gets rid of the salt that enters its system by expelling it through its leaves. One can test this scientific marvel most unscientifically by licking a finger, running it over any of the tree's dark green leaves, and then licking it once again. Since your finger will taste very salty, this little experiment should not be conducted on a hot day when you are already dying of thirst.

During the summer months, the Black Mangrove's small but profuse flowers attract swarms of bees. The end result of their attraction is a white honey that is sold under the name "Mangrove Honey."

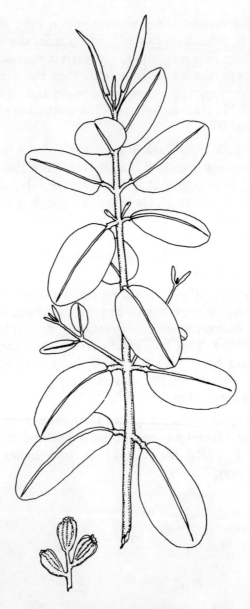

WHITE MANGROVE

White Mangrove
Laguncularia racemosa

Moving a bit farther inland, one finds the White Mangrove growing about 30' tall in what is called the intertidal zone. Once again, the tree's leaves are largely responsible for its survival in a salt-water environment under a scorching, subtropical sun.

The leaves of the White Mangrove, like those of so many native species, have a thick, varnish-like coating that enables them to resist being dried out by the sun and, at the same time, retain precious moisture. Moreover, the tree expels deadly salt through two tiny glands located at the very base of its leaves, a characteristic shared by the Button Mangrove that thrives in the next inland zone. (See Chapter 5 for further discussion of the Button Mangrove.)

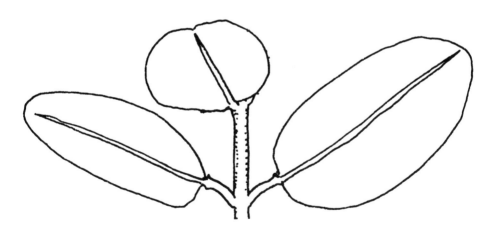

CHAPTER 7.

THE COLORFUL EXOTICS

Although Sanibel's native vegetation is blessed with many commendable attributes, vivid color is not normally one of them. Thus in an effort to relieve the relative monotony of several shades of green in this earthly Eden, colorful exotics are planted around our resorts, retail stores, restaurants and residences. While the word "exotic" sounds incredibly romantic, and even slightly sinful, Sanibel's definition of exotic flora merely refers to plants that have been introduced by Man and are not native to southern Florida.

Despite the fact that so many exotics require watering and fertilizing on a barrier island where fresh water is a precious resource and fertilizers are harmful to the environment, the City of Sanibel recognizes the demand for colorful relief. Thus while our local government strongly encourages the planting of native species, it tolerates the introduction of "non-competing exotics," i.e., plants that pose no threat to native vegetation.

When I moved to Sanibel in 1978, I was quite shocked to learn that all the beautiful Bougainvillea, Hibiscus, and countless other colorful plants that everyone associates with tropical isles were not native. On the contrary, they originally came from faraway places like South America, the Mediterranean, Madagascar and, believe it or not, China! However, many exotics thrive on Sanibel because our climate is similar to that of their native homelands, and the knowledge of their true origins in no way diminishes one's delight in their presence.

This chapter is devoted to the most colorful and conspicuous "non-competing exotics" that every visitor will certainly see and admire. Since no black and white illustration could possibly do justice to the beauty of these plants, one will find them all in the color section of this book.

BOUGAINVILLEA

It seems highly appropriate to begin a discussion of exotics with Bougainvillea, for it is one of the most beautiful and popular shrubs. While those with crimson blooms seem to be particularly prized, one may also see purple or salmon specimens on Sanibel. In any event and in any color, however, the Bougainvillea's "bracts" always surround three, tiny white flowers.

Although the brilliant Bougainvillea is a native of Brazil, it was named after Louis Antoine de Bougainville, an 18th century French noble and navigator. A man of many talents, de Bougainville wrote a treatise on integral calculus at the age of 25, served as aide-de-camp to the ill-fated Marquis de Montcalm in Canada, and subsequently distinguished himself in the Seven Years' War.

When the Bourbon monarchy cast covetous eyes on the Falkland Islands, de Bougainville undertook to colonize them at his own expense, an extraordinary form of patriotism of which the Spaniards took an exceedingly dim view that prevailed over the Frenchman's ardor. Shortly thereafter, the indomitable de Bougainville set forth on a two-year voyage of discovery around the world. However, his eagerness to conduct an expedition to the North Pole met with a frigid reception at the Bourbon court.

By some miracle, de Bougainville escaped Robespierre's guillotine during the Reign of Terror, and was subsequently made a senator and a member of the Legion of Honor by Napoleon. In view of the French aristocrat's distinguished and highly colorful career, the South American genus containing about a dozen vivid shrubs immortalizes his name.

HIBISCUS

Like Bougainvillea, Hibiscus is an extremely popular shrub in tropical regions. An evergreen that blooms throughout the year, its large, bell-shaped flowers may be single or double, and are usually red, orange, yellow, pink or white. Although the brilliant blooms open at dawn and fall to the ground by dusk, the Hibiscus always greets the following day with a full array of fresh flowers.

A native of China, *Hibiscus* is the largest genus of the extraordinarily prolific mallow family that boasts 45 genera and some

900 species! While the genus *Gossypium* (cotton) has far greater economic value than all the ornamental species of the genus *Hibiscus*, the latter is clearly the family favorite in terms of beauty and is the official flower of Hawaii.

Although Hibiscus cannot compete with cotton in terms of economic importance, its fallen blooms grace the dinner tables of many island homes. In Jamaica, the shrub is often called Shoe Flower by those who use its petals to shine their shoes.

SEA HIBISCUS (MAHOE)

Although the Sea Hibiscus is clearly a tree and not a shrub, it belongs to the same family as Hibiscus and thus shares the latter's distinguished lineage. Like the flowers of the Hibiscus, the tree's bell-shaped blooms are born in the morning and die at dusk. In the process of going from infancy to maturity to senility in the same day, however, the flowers undergo a radical transformation that once caused considerable dissension among *Homo sapiens* on Sanibel.

While jogging towards the beach one morning, I happened to overhear a heated argument at a Gulf-front resort between a husband and his wife. The former pointed to the yellow flowers on a Sea Hibiscus and declared that his spouse must have been soused the previous afternoon when she claimed to have seen red flowers on the tree in question. Although the woman looked extremely puzzled, she insisted that the flowers had indeed been red, and that her preprandial libations had most certainly not induced hallucinations!

Although joggers are loath to disrupt their rhythm, I made an exception in the case of the contentious couple in order to restore some measure of connubial bliss. Thus I told them that they were *both* right, for the flowers of the Sea Hibiscus are yellow in the morning, generally turn orange by noon, and become blood red before dying in the afternoon.

IXORA (FLAME OF THE WOODS)

People who visit Sanibel during the off-season are sometimes disappointed to find little more than shell scrap on the famous beaches of "the shell capital of the world." However, the fact that many of our most beautiful exotics are in full bloom during the late spring and summer months may be a consolation prize, if one is willing to turn one's attention from shells to shrubs.

The exotic Ixora from India greets off-season visitors with a profusion of brilliant red flowers (about ¾" across) that clearly merit the plant's common name, Flame of the Woods. While the shrub may grow nearly 10' high, it is usually trimmed considerably in order to encourage dense clusters of blooms.

ROYAL POINCIANA

Like Ixora, the magnificent Royal Poinciana reserves its crowning glory for the benefit of off-season visitors. Thus those who arrive in the late spring or early summer will certainly admire the South American tree's scarlet blooms and fine, feathery leaves. While many Islanders have planted Royal Poincianas in their yards, the superb specimens at St. Michael's Episcopal Church on Periwinkle Way, and those at the Shalimar Hotel on West Gulf Drive, enjoy particularly high visibility.

Apart from those weeks of flaming color, however, the Royal Poinciana is bare and leafless during a good part of the year. Indeed, all one sees for many months is a number of long, dark, dangling pods, a rather unattractive reminder that the tree belongs to the large legume family.

OLEANDER

A tall, flowering shrub from the Mediterranean region, Oleander is frequently planted along roads and around homes and resorts throughout Florida. While the plant blooms for most of the year, its flowers are especially profuse in the late winter and throughout the spring when red, pink and white are the colors that one is most likely to see on Sanibel.

Unfortunately, Nature occasionally indulges in the rather perverse pleasure of creating something that is both beautiful and deadly. So far as Oleander is concerned, *all* parts of the plant are poisonous. Thus cattle have become seriously ill by munching on the shrub's glossy green leaves that contain a poisonous, milky juice. Moreover, island naturalist George Campbell reports that a young boy died after eating marshmallows toasted on an Oleander twig!

The Greeks and Romans were very familiar with Oleander, and Pliny described the plant's poisonous potential as well as its beautiful blooms. Although few of us plough through Pliny these days, we should be well aware of the fact that Oleander is just as beautiful and just as deadly today as it was in ancient times.

PERIWINKLE

Most people, including a number of Islanders, assume that the small Periwinkle is a native plant since it grows wild in many parts of Florida. Moreover, Sanibel's main thoroughfare is called Periwinkle Way, a distinction that almost suggests an official seal of approval by a city that smiles upon natives and frowns upon exotics.

In fact, however, Periwinkle appears to grow wild only because it reseeds itself, a few old-time Islanders insist that our main artery was really named after the lowly Periwinkle snail, and the plant itself is a native of Madagascar. To be sure, none of the preceding diminishes one's pleasure in seeing the rosy purple or white flowers that bloom throughout the year on a plant that is not even 2' tall. Those who visit the Conservation Center will certainly find Periwinkle at the base of the Observation Tower and, most appropriately, the plant embellishes the entrance to a major shopping center, Periwinkle Place.

Since Nature is supremely fickle, some of her lovely creations may be very harmful to mankind (*e.g.*, Oleander), while others may be extemely beneficial. The Madagascar Periwinkle ranks very high on the list of Nature's benevolent bounty, for it appears that this modest little plant produces an alkaloid that has been quite effective in treating certain kinds of cancer. The drug has been cleared by the U.S.D.A. and is marketed by a major pharmaceutical firm.

102

CHAPTER 8.

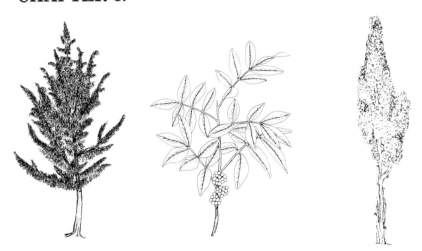

THE TERRIBLE TRIO

While many of Florida's imported exotics provide colorful relief from the dominant greens of native species, the introduction of three beautiful trees around the turn of the century was tantamount to opening Pandora's box, although no one realized it at that time. Today, however, ecologists are keenly aware of the clear and present danger posed by Australian Pine, Brazilian Pepper, and Melaleuca.

It is indeed a fact that the terrible trio of "weed trees" or "noxious plants" threatens to overwhelm native vegetation, since the former are prodigiously prolific and generally grow faster and taller than Sanibel's indigenous plants. Thus native species must plead *nolo contendere* in the race for a place in the sun and, as a result, die in the shade of the alien invaders.

Initially, and quite understandably, one might not mourn the demise of plants that are primarily green and generally not very exciting to look at. But should the "weed trees" succeed in crowding out native species, Sanibel could no longer attract or sustain the astonishing variety of wildlife that makes it such a special, Sanctuary Island. Many of the migrating birds, for example, would simply turn up their beaks in disgust and winter elsewhere!

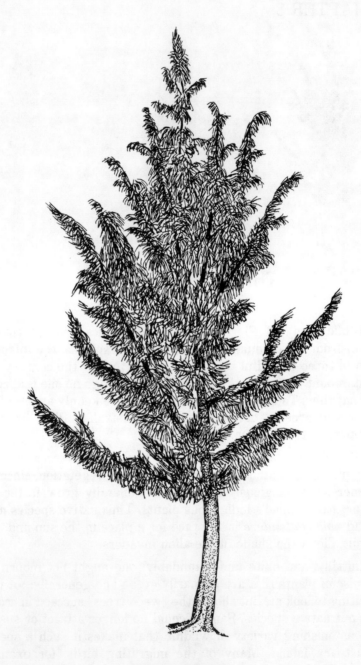

AUSTRALIAN PINE

AUSTRALIAN PINE
Casuarina equisetifolia

Despite its common name and appearance, the magnificent Australian Pine is a *Casuarina* and not a pine, a botanical technicality that provides a degree of edification without diminishing one's admiration for the towering tree that may grow 150' tall. Everyone enjoys the "Periwinkle Tunnel" formed by those trees on Sanibel's main thoroughfare, not to mention their welcome shade along many beaches.

Prior to World War I, the Australian Pine was brought to Sanibel for the purpose of providing a windbreak on island farms and a suitable ornamental for a few main roads. By the mid-1950s, however, the scattering of vast numbers of seeds had enabled the tree to extend its domain well beyond its assigned territory, an inexorable invasion that continues to this day.

Since Australian Pines tend to grow close together in rather dense stands, they easily overwhelm native plants that do not normally grow so quickly and can never compete for sunlight with the alien's superior height. Moreover, the tree's needle-like leaves fall to the ground and create a smothering blanket that often inhibits the growth of native species.

Although the tree develops a very respectable tap root and root system in its native Australia, it seems too lazy to do so on Sanibel, probably because fresh water lies just a few feet below the ground. Thus hurricane winds, or even those of violent storms, easily uproot the trees and toss them onto roads that are both our daily lifeline and our evacuation routes.

"Beefwood" and "Ironwood" are terms that are sometimes applied to the Australian Pine. The former refers to the fact that the tree's wood has a lovely, reddish hue, while the latter indicates that one must be willing to ruin many saw blades and haul away extraordinarily heavy chunks in order to make anything from that beautiful wood.

BRAZILIAN PEPPER (FLORIDA HOLLY)
Schinus terebinthifolius

Unlike other members of the terrible trio, Brazilian Pepper does not tower over the tallest native species. However, it more than compensates for that disadvantage by virtue of extremely rapid growth, extraordinarily wide dispersal (thanks primarily to greedy birds), and a singular resistance to Man's attempts to administer extreme unction.

Brazilian Pepper was brought to Florida during the latter part of the nineteenth century. The fast-growing tree was both immediately and immensely popular, and many horticulturists declared that no self-respecting garden was complete without the shiny green leaves and bright red berries of the exotic "Florida Holly." In the mid-1950s, when Sanibel was on the threshold of massive development, Brazilian Peppers were few and far between. Today, alas, they are everywhere. Although developers and homeowners planted some of the trees as ornamentals, their ubiquitous presence on this island is primarily due to the gluttony of birds, robins in particular.

Many species of migrating birds have wintered on Sanibel for countless years. However, it was only when Brazilian Peppers became so woefully well established that robins really discovered this barrier island. Thus during the winter season, many a robin gorges on the tree's berries to such an extent that it staggers around the ground in a seemingly drunken stupor and finds it impossible to fly off with such a heavy cargo.

Should such a stuffed robin not fall prey to a feral feline, or to some other wild creature, it eventually becomes airborne and jettisons undigested seeds willy-nilly. While one is no longer allowed to plant Brazilian Peppers on Sanibel, and anyone seeking a development permit must remove all those weed trees from his property, such legislation has absolutely no impact on the digestive tract of a bird!

Ecologists are primarily concerned, and rightly so, by the insidious threat that Brazilian Pepper poses to native vegetation. However, everyone should be aware of the fact that the exotic from Brazil may also be quite harmful to mankind. For example, one would be well advised not to deck the halls with boughs of Florida Holly. The tree is related to Poison Ivy, and some people who touch it break out in a horrid, itchy rash.

Moreover, *terebinthifolius* refers to the fact that the tree's crushed leaves smell like turpentine, a highly unpleasant olfactory sensation that once caused a young man to faint for 15 minutes at the Conservation Center! In addition to relating the true story of that hapless young man, Arthur Clark, the Center's peerless botanical guide, speaks of an interesting article that appeared in *The Wall Street Journal* a few years ago. It seems that several posh, New York restaurants imported something called "Pink Pepper" from France, with the result that a number of their clientele suffered severe indigestion and, in a few instances, temporary lung arrest. A subsequent analysis of the new culinary sensation proved that Pink Pepper was none other than the dried and ground berries of the Brazilian Pepper.

MELALEUCA

MELALEUCA (CAJEPUT, PAPERBARK, PUNK TREE)
Melaleuca quinquenervia

In 1984, the extremely handsome Melaleuca tree caused a storm of highly emotional controversy on Sanibel and became a veritable *cause célèbre* that inspired countless letters to the editors of both island newspapers. While the City wished to enforce eradication of that Australian exotic, many citizens were appalled by the very idea of imposing a death sentence on such a beautiful tree that, unlike Brazilian Pepper, currently posed no *visible* threat to native vegetation on Sanibel.

The City lost the first round in what became known as "The Melaleuca Melee." However, Sanibel's Noxious Plant Control Officer subsequently sent both a letter and a bulletin on the weed tree to every resident who harbored so much as a single specimen on his property. In essence, homeowners were informed that "Melaleuca poses a very real threat to the ecological integrity of Sanibel" because it is "a biological 'time bomb' capable of completely taking over natural vegetative communities." Few homeowners elected to have their lovely Melaleucas removed, at the City's expense.

The Melaleuca was brought to southern Florida in the early 1900s and was frequently planted as an ornamental. However, the arrival of Melaleucas happened to coincide with the prevailing view that all of southern Florida's buggy swamps and wetlands should be drained and dried up. Since the Melaleuca was known to consume prodigious amounts of water, countless thousands of its seeds were scattered with gay abandon in swampy or wetland areas.

Today, one of the largest stands of pure Melaleuca is in the vicinity of the Koreshan Unity Park for, some 75 years ago, the editor of the official publication of the Koreshan Unity religious group took it upon himself to scatter Melaleuca seeds all over that area in the sincere conviction that he was doing southern Florida a great favor. Indeed, Melaleuca has thrived to such a degree that over 40,000 acres south of Lake Okeechobee are now pure Melaleuca!

Unfortunately, southern Florida is now faced with a *fait accompli* at a time when scientists convincingly argue that the destruction of swamps and wetlands spells the destruction of Florida's natural ecology, and that certain exotic invaders further threaten ecological integrity by crowding out native species. So far as Sanibel is concerned, ecologists are convinced that Melaleucas pose a real threat to the interior wetlands, the kind of environment in which those greedy guzzlers of fresh or brackish water thrive. Their invasion of our vital wetlands is already under way and, should it continue unchecked, ecologists fear that Melaleucas might eventually dry up the wetlands to a considerable degree, crowd out native vegetation, and deprive a great variety of wildlife of their natural habitat.

Those who study ways of eliminating the harmful alien invader are faced with a Herculean task. In short, how does one go about killing a tree that clings to life so tenaciously and, every year after the age of three, may produce nearly 20 million tiny seeds that fly through the air with the greatest of ease? Fire does not seem to bother the Melaleuca very much, for its thick, cork-like bark generally protects it from severe damage. Cutting it down only serves to inspire the majority of Melaleuca stumps to sprout and start life all over again and, should one attempt to dig out those stumps, the tree's last gasp may well be the explosion of countless thousands of seeds!

While modern research clearly indicates that the Australian exotic poses a distinct threat to the ecological integrity of southern Florida, several studies have concluded that there's money to be made from Melaleucas. The wood could provide good stakes for Florida's vast fields of tomato plants, the pulp might be useful in the paper industry, and a Fort Myers firm is currently harvesting the peeling bark for use as a mulch and potting soil. Thus should it prove impossible to eliminate or control the Melaleuca, one may at least derive some benefit from its pernicious presence.

CHAPTER 9.

INTRODUCTION

Since the animal kingdom includes insects, there are undoubtedly more species of animals than plants on Sanibel. Indeed, according to one authority, there may be about 100 species
of moths and butterflies flitting about this barrier island! While
many of our butterflies and other insects are strikingly beautiful,
one has to admit that Sanibel is also the home of certain species
(flying piranhas like mosquitoes and No-See-Ums) that are
singularly lacking in redeeming features so far as mankind is
concerned.

In view of the fact that Florida's "bugs" are most certainly
not a tourist attraction, and only a dedicated entomologist
might be truly enamored of them, the following chapters will be
devoted to those larger members of the animal kingdom that
everyone enjoys seeing on Sanibel. Snakes are excluded only
because so many people (including this author) go out of their
way to avoid rather than to admire them, a fact that in no way
diminishes their value or indeed their beauty in the eyes of
braver beholders.

Although Sanibel is a Sanctuary Island on which wildlife is
protected, the pitiful roadside remains of raccoons, turtles,
snakes and armadillos bear silent testimony to Man's failure to
slow down. Since so many of our resident wild animals are nocturnal, they are especially vulnerable to speeding cars at night.
Careful daytime drivers, on the other hand, may be richly
rewarded by stopping to lend a helping hand to a Gopher Tortoise
as it crawls across a busy island road.

CHAPTER 10.

THE KEY WEST FLAP FLASHER
(Key West Anole)

The alligator is clearly a major tourist attraction; the Anole is certainly not. However, since one must generally make some effort to find the former but absolutely none to locate the latter, it seems logical to begin a discussion of Sanibel's wild animals with the little, leaping lizard.

Indeed, Anoles are ubiquitous. They scamper all over the ground, crawl up and down trees, scurry along porch screens, float majestically on leaves in swimming pools, and streak across tennis courts as though defying players to call a let for a lizard. Although the Green Anole is native, it is now so rare that one is most likely to see the Key West Anole, a grayish-brown lizard of similar size and habits.

A native of the Bahamas, the Key West Anole may have arrived in Key West and made its way to Sanibel courtesy of potted plants. Subsequently, the alien Anole not only usurped the Green Anole's place in the Sanibel sun but, according to one observer, ate it as well! However, the unregistered alien generally feasts on small insects, some of which are most undesirable native residents.

It is always amusing to observe the antics of the Key West Anole when it pauses to do pushups, an athletic feat that is frequently accompanied by repeated inflations of the bright orange flap below its throat. Scientists speculate that flashing the flap may be the lizard's way of attracting a mate or intimidating a predator. However, having observed for many years the pushups and flap-flashing propensities of countless Anoles when neither predators nor potential brides were present, I strongly suspect that much of the flap flashing is merely an exuberant expression of *joie de vivre.*

CHAPTER 11.
THE INFLATABLE TANK
(Nine-Banded Armadillo)

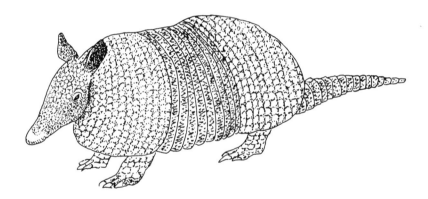

ARMADILLO

It is often said that seeing is believing, and the armadillo is certainly a case in point! The strange-looking creature, averaging just over 2' in length and weighing about 10 pounds, is almost completely covered by three sections of what appear to be armored plates, but are actually extremely tough skin. Indeed, the armadillo's most vulnerable spot is its soft underside, which boasts but a few, scraggly hairs.

Like sloths and anteaters, the primitive armadillo belongs to the *Edentata* order whose members are not supposed to have any teeth, although some do and the armadillo is one of them. However, the small pegs that pass for teeth are not at all crucial to the survival of the little armored animal that is so well protected by its carapace and by its ability to burrow away from danger with incredible speed, thanks to extremely sharp claws.

Given its elongated muzzle, exceedingly long tongue, and sharp claws, the armadillo is admirably equipped to forage for the food that it finds particularly delectable: bugs. Certainly no one objects when the creature laps up termites or an entire colony of ants in no time at all, especially if the latter are fire ants. However, Islanders who harbor mole crickets on their property frequently wake up to find that, during the night, an armadillo has left a lot of holes and little piles of dirt on their well-tended lawns.

Since there were no armadillos on Sanibel until the early 1960s, a period that just happened to coincide with the completion of the Causeway, it is conceivable that a few of those nocturnal creatures crossed the Causeway under cover of darkness without stopping to pay the toll. However, it is far more likely that our armadillos swam across the bay.

While the origins of the Nine-Banded Armadillo's immigration are somewhat obscure, it appears that entire panzer divisions moved from Mexico in the mid-1880s. They scurried north but, with no fur to protect them from the cold, many turned east and some eventually arrived in Florida after World War I. Obviously, the Rio Grande and the mighty Mississippi did not pose insurmountable problems for the inflatable armadillo!

Should an armadillo wish to cross a canal or something like the Sanibel River, it is apparently quite capable of walking under water on the bottom. When faced with larger expanses, like San Carlos Bay, the creature swallows quantities of air in order to inflate its intestines and stomach, thereby rendering it sufficiently buoyant to float across, perhaps thrashing a bit with its feet.

Unfortunately, Man poses the greatest threat to the survival of an ancient animal that has few enemies. In several parts of our nation, armadillos are hunted and roasted; some compare the flavor of their flesh to chicken, others to pork. In view of their constant burrowing, farmers often shoot armadillos on sight, while some people kill them in order to peddle their carapaces as curiosities.

Although armadillos are protected by law on Sanibel, the only armadillo that one is likely to see here is a squashed specimen by the road. Since the creature leaps into the air when alarmed, speeding cars invariably score a direct hit. Thus to this date, CROW has not been able to treat an injured armadillo and restore it to the wild, for the hapless creature is usually DOA (dead on arrival).

Since armadillos are nocturnal by nature, motorists are by no means entirely responsible for one's difficulty in sighting a live specimen. However, as indicated earlier, the creatures are not equipped to cope with cold weather. Thus it was not until Christmas Day in 1983, when the temperature was in the mid-20s, that I finally saw a live armadillo happily digging holes in someone's lawn under the relatively warm sun.

Given its primitive brain, the armadillo is certainly not noted for its intelligence, and its vision is so poor that it has been known to bump into people and the side of a barn, repeatedly. However, there is something rather endearing about a harmless creature that looks like a toy tank from another planet. Moreover, anyone who appreciates order will certainly applaud the armadillo's reproductive habits. After mating in the summer, the female always produces four, miniature armored replicas, all of the same sex. What? Never so much as a single maverick? Well, hardly ever.

CHAPTER 12.

AN AQUATIC RABBIT
(Marsh Rabbit)

A few years ago, I happened to be in the Conservation Center's gift shop when an English couple excitedly inquired about a very strange creature that they had seen at "Ding" Darling. Given the highly detailed and wonderfully articulate description of the English visitors, a volunteer guide informed them that they had probably seen a Marsh Rabbit. "Well," conceded the wife most gracefully, "Harold rather thought that it might have been some species of rabbit, even though it lacked a proper tail!"

Certainly our Marsh Rabbit is no one's idea of a proper Peter Rabbit-cum-cottontail. Indeed, the Marsh Rabbit's brownish tail is so small that it is often hard to see it at all. Although Sanibel's lean, brownish rabbit boasts no white, and its tail, ears, and hind feet are shorter than those of specimens that one is used to seeing, the creature certainly looks and behaves like a bona fide rabbit, much to the annoyance of Island gardeners.

For six months in 1982, I was fortunate enough to "sit" in the lovely bayside home of Snowbird friends from Indiana. Thus I had a fine opportunity to observe many Marsh Rabbits along Dixie Beach Boulevard, a straight road nearly two miles long that goes from Periwinkle Way to San Carlos Bay. Residential communities line the east side of the road, while "Ding" Darling occupies a good portion of the west side.

Since Marsh Rabbits seem to thrive around brackish waters and the swampy regions where mangroves reign supreme, I invariably saw at least a dozen of them nibbling away at the grass by both sides of the road on which I jogged every morning. At first, the rabbits fled when I approached. However, they soon realized that the due and most deliberate speed with which 'that dumb blond' plodded along posed no threat whatsoever, with the result that I watched them nibble while they watched me sweat.

In addition to more than the usual quota of mosquitoes, rain, and the threat of a hurricane that became "disorganized" at the eleventh hour, the summer of 1982 will long be remembered for the infamous "No-Name Storm." That unheralded onslaught unleashed the Rains of Ranchipur on Sanibel and rendered several parts of the island inaccessible, except by boat. Apart from worrying about the waters lapping at the foundations of the home that I was supposed to protect, I had most unpleasant visions of scores of drowned Marsh Rabbits.

When the waters finally receded, I steeled myself for the sight of countless corpses as I jogged along Dixie Beach Boulevard. However, all I saw was an inordinate amount of debris and the usual contingent of Marsh Rabbits nibbling voraciously in the grass. Since Marsh Rabbits are fine swimmers and, according to island naturalist George Campbell, can easily cover over 1,000', the aquatic rabbits had simply swum to higher ground.

While motorists take a very heavy toll of wildlife, I have seen only two Marsh Rabbits that *may* have been killed by cars during seven years of jogging all over this island. Thus it would seem that the Marsh Rabbit is able to co-exist with Man and survive very well on Sanibel. However, the creature is not without enemies, and feral felines probably head the list.

CHAPTER 13.

PHYLLIS THE FERAL FELINE
(Wild Cat)

Island newspapers frequently refer to feral felines and occasionally, in an effort to find a loving home for a particularly appealing or pathetic specimen, include a picture. Out-of-state readers are often puzzled by all the ado over a creature that looks exactly like a common cat but which, for some strange reason, Islanders call a feral feline.

A feral feline is just a wild cat, and not some kind of wildcat. The only difference between a wild cat and its more fortunate domestic relatives is the fact that the former lives in the wild and has thus become quite wild as a result.

No one knows exactly how many feral felines live on Sanibel, but it is safe to say that there are scores of them. Moreover, no one knows precisely how long they have been here, although it is eminently clear that their population has grown by leaps and bounds since the completion of the Causeway in 1963. I hasten to add that countless cats have not been slinking across the Causeway (toll free) for over twenty years! Rather, a great many arrived as cuddly kittens in the comfortable cars of misguided people who felt that their unwanted litters would enjoy the good life on Sanibel, as opposed to the caged life at the local Humane Society.

Whenever survival is at stake, any domestic cat can become a wild cat in no time at all, whether it be abandoned as a kitten or as an adult reared on Tender Vittles and regular visits to the vet. Unfortunately, such feral felines are alien invaders that pose a considerable threat to wildlife on Sanibel since their indiscriminate diet includes little lizards, small snakes, young Marsh Rabbits, baby birds, *etc.* In addition to finding sufficient sustenance on Sanibel, wild cats propagate prodigiously!

While many feral felines flee from *Homo sapiens*, some are clever enough to recognize a patsy when they see one, even if he is the giant king of the animal kingdom. Thus people are often tempted to feed a consummate cat con artist whose mere presence vividly portrays a sad saga of malnutrition, mistreatment, and the total deprivation of any tender loving care. Should you not be fully convinced, there is always the mournful "Meow." Brace yourself!

If you are not prepared to adopt until death do you part, *never* feed a feral feline. However, if you are willing to pay through the nose for sickness rather than health and feel richer for being poorer, then by all means adopt a wild cat — and have it spayed (or neutered) right after it laps up its first bowl of milk.

Frankly, I have never really cared for cats. They shed their hair all over the house, sharpen their claws on the furniture, and seem to have a distinct aversion to scoring a direct hit *within* the generous confines of a litter box. So what does one do when a scrawny feral feline clings to the porch screen during a raging storm and, of course, contrives to look totally helpless, utterly devoid of hope, and ripe for imminent extinction in the gaping maw of an errant alligator? Well, whether you like cats or not, you may be adopted for the duration.

Thus it came to pass that a friend and I were adopted by a very weird-looking wild cat whose extraordinarily long, striped tail really belonged on a raccoon. In addition, her hair was of different lengths and stood out in every conceivable direction as though charged by electricity, and great tufts of unruly hair sprouted from her ears as well. We named her after that zany comedienne, whose hair also defies both description and the law of gravity, Phyllis Diller.

Ms. Diller was duly spayed and given the proper number of shots. Over the years, she has hissed and bared her fangs whenever the vet checks for the presence of worms, and absolutely refuses to swallow her flea pill unless it is liberally coated wtih Land O Lakes butter. Moreover, should the culinary concoctions of Crave, 9 Lives, Fancy Feast or Pounce fail to meet with Ms. Diller's fickle approval, she abandons them to the ants and stalks off in a fit of pique to reduce Sanibel's wildlife population by hunting little lizards, snakes, frogs, *etc.*

Alas, Phyllis the Feral Feline, *et al.*, will always be a menace to wildlife on Sanibel. Moreover, since one can never trust even a semi-domesticated wild cat, the failure to be wary may well result in severe scratches that require tetanus shots.

CHAPTER 14.

THE LOVABLE LANDLORD
(Gopher Tortoise)

Since "gopher" comes from an old French verb meaning to tunnel, the term is applied to three different groups of burrowing animals: the small rodents called gophers or pocket gophers, a number of striped ground squirrels and, of course, the lovable land tortoise. The Gopher Tortoise digs a splendid tunnel, a few feet deep and many yards long, that it generously shares with a variety of wildlife without charging its tenants a cent!

On this resort island, the Gopher Tortoise's rent-free tenants may include rabbits, rodents, opossums, and snakes. While most of Sanibel's serpents are not poisonous, there are a few rattlers and coral snakes slithering around, and thus one is well advised to follow the example of a visiting scientist who examined the creature's burrow with the aid of mirrors.

Since millions of children are familiar with the delightful fable about the tortoise and the hare, millions of adults dread the day when their offspring put away childish things and innocently inquire, "What's the difference between a tortoise and a turtle?" Fortunately, turtles and tortoises belong to the same order, *Chelonia*, and it is now considered quite acceptable to use the two terms interchangeably.

However, some scientists still insist that while all tortoises are turtles not all turtle are tortoises, since a tortoise is a turtle that lives on land. Thus according to that mind-boggling definition, the Gopher Tortoise claims the distinction of being the last true tortoise in this general region. Unfortunately, the timid vegetarian that holds such a distinction may some day be faced with the threat of extinction.

Zoologists at the University of Florida estimate that the Gopher Tortoise population has been reduced by about 75 percent. While the harmless creature is currently listed as a species of special concern, many hope that it will soon be classified as threatened before it joins the ranks of the unfortunate elite on the endangered list. Alas, the Gopher Tortoise must contend with both Man and Nature.

Since a mature Gopher Tortoise weighs about 10 pounds and can quickly withdraw into a protective shell that may be over a foot long, one has to wonder what the reptile has to fear from Nature's other wild creatures — even though it forages for food in broad daylight. In fact, a *mature* Gopher Tortoise has little to fear from any other wild animal, with the exception of *Homo sapiens*. However, surviving until the age of maturity is an extremely precarious proposition.

Unlike rabbits, feral felines, and many other animals, the Gopher Tortoise is a model of restraint when it comes to reproduction. Indeed, it must survive in the wild for some 16 years before making a stab at ensuring the survival of the species. Then, when a female is finally able to mate and produce perhaps half a dozen eggs, about 80 percent of her miniature offspring never make it to maturity, generally because they are such tasty hors d'oeuvres for raccoons and all manner of wild creatures.

Certainly the problems related to reproduction and survival described in the preceding paragraph are part of the natural order of things. However, Man's intervention in modern times is largely responsible for the sharp decline in the Gopher Tortoise population of our southeastern states, where the creature is still hunted for food and where developers bulldoze its burrows.

Surely no one would fault the Calusa Indians for eating Gopher Tortoises or point an accusing finger at hungry victims of the Great Depression, for whom Gopher Tortoises (called "Hoover Chickens" or "Georgia Bacon") often meant the difference between starvation and survival. While Gopher Tortoise stew was frequently served in Sanibel's restaurants, such is no longer the case since wildlife is protected on this Sanctuary Island. However, eating fried Gopher at a church supper is a tradition in many parts of the southeastern United States, and it is extremely difficult to persuade people to abandon a time-honored custom.

Oddly enough, Gopher Tortoises and developers have something in common: they both prefer high, dry ground, an increasingly rare commodity in Florida. Thus countless burrows have been bulldozed in order to make way for countless condos. As a result, only a few Gopher Tortoise colonies now remain on Sanibel. One of those, located on the property of the old Casa Ybel airstrip, was saved in 1984 when the City of Sanibel denied a request for a golf course-cum-condos on that site.

When you drive along our roads during the day, you may well see a Gopher Tortoise attempting to make its way across a busy thoroughfare at the painfully slow pace of a snail. Those who stop to lend the gentle creature a helping hand to safety will be richly rewarded by the knowledge that even such a small contribution may mean the difference between survival and extinction.

CHAPTER 15.

SANIBEL DISPOSAL
(Raccoon)

Since raccoons roam all over the United States, most people are very familiar with the rather chunky creature whose black-and-white ringed tail adorns the warm coonskin hats and car aerials of Daniel Boone's descendants. Even my octogenarian mother, who can never throw anything away, still sports her full-length raccoon coat that was all the rage on college campuses in the 1920s.

Whether for food, for fur, or just for fun, it seems that Americans have always hunted raccoons. Indeed, some hunters even have specially trained "coon dogs" for that purpose. Since coon hunting is practiced throughout the nation, one would certainly expect raccoons to be on the endangered species list. In fact, however, they are currently not endangered, threatened, or even considered to be a species of special concern!

While most wild animals suffer from the inexorable encroachments of human civilization, raccoons have managed to adapt to such a degree that they actually thrive in close proximity to *Homo sapiens.* This is largely due to the fact that Man has an infinite capacity to produce garbage, and raccoons have a commensurate capacity to consume it.

Theoretically, raccoons are carnivorous. In fact, however, they are voraciously omnivorous. In addition to eating mice, baby birds and turtles, frogs, and all manner of seafood, they fight over nuts, the berries of the Cabbage Palm, and garbage galore. Since raccoons combine great curiosity with remarkable manual dexterity, they head the list of Nature's nuisances on Sanibel. After all, a creature that is capable of prying open an oyster has little difficulty in prying open a garbage can, unscrewing a lid, or opening an unlocked door.

One island friend has contended with raccoons in her attic for several years at considerable expense, while another acquaintance found that a powerful light and a bucket of cold water failed to deter an amorous couple of coons from pitching woo on her porch. And, of course, many Islanders must rise, shine, and set out their garbage at the crack of dawn lest raccoons deprive Sanibel Disposal of its just deserts.

The life style of Sanibel's raccoons is somewhat different from that of their northern relatives, who generally hibernate during the winter and are normally nocturnal. Surely there is no need to go into hibernation on a subtropical island and, if low tides expose all kinds of delicacies at dawn or at dusk, the raccoon is quite willing to adjust its internal clock accordingly! Thus many Islanders who live by canals have seen raccoons fighting over "coon oysters," a battle that is invariably accompanied by much hissing and screeching in stereophonic sound.

Car kills take a heavy toll of raccoons and one is certainly tempted to feed young kits that appear to be orphans, for there is no denying the fact that such creatures look very cute and cuddly. However, they are definitely not at all cuddly, they are quick to bite, and are major carriers of rabies.

On the whole, it is not a good idea to feed any wild animal lest it lose its healthy fear of humans and its ability to survive in the wild. Should you come across any species of wildlife that appears to be injured or orphaned, the best thing to do is to call CROW (Care and Rehabilitation of Wildlife), 472-3644.

OPOSSUM WITH YOUNG

124

CHAPTER 16.

BRAINS AREN'T EVERYTHING
(Opossum)

Quite apart from the fact that neither the furry opossum nor the armored armadillo would ever win a wildlife beauty contest, the two primitive creatures have many other things in common. The only representatives of their respective orders in the United States, both nocturnal mammals first appeared on Sanibel after the completion of the Causeway in 1963. Moreover, these animals are so very primitive and endowed with such limited gray matter that they seem far too dumb to compete with creatures of much higher intelligence, especially their major enemy, Man the hunter or Man the driver. Fortunately, brains aren't everything and both animals boast an admirable record of survival against the odds.

Since the opossum has a marsupium or pouch, it belongs to the *Marsupialia* order that includes kangaroos, koala bears, and wombats, Measuring some 3′ in length, including a whitish tail tinged with pink that accounts for roughly one third of that dimension, a mature opossum is covered with grayish, furry hair (except for the tail). One is not likely to spot a live opossum on Sanibel for the unsociable creature is nocturnal by nature and, when not out foraging for food, hides in a hole in the ground or up in a tree. Unfortunately, one may well see hapless victims along island roads.

The survival of opossum offspring is one of Nature's major miracles. Brought forth into an unfriendly world barely two weeks after conception, some 18-20 blind, deaf and hairless opossums are little more than minute embryos, each weighing about 1/2800 of a pound! They must immediately seek safety and sustenance by climbing up into their mother's pouch. Having completed the arduous, 3″ ascent, a number of offspring find that survival is a matter of first come first served, for the mother has only 13 teats.

While the lucky thirteen cling tenaciously to the nourishing teats for about two months, one has to wonder about the quality of a childhood spent in an opossum's pouch. Although I have read that an expecting opossum cleans out her pouch prior to the arrival of her progeny, I can find no reference to any further concern for cleanliness during the two months that her offspring are in residence.

Despite an environment that is high on carbon dioxide and unseemly *et cetera*, little opossums crawl out of the pouch and spend about another six weeks with their mother. Sometimes they grab the fur on her back and hitchhike, while at other times they cling by their tails to her tail. Indeed, the opossum claims the distinction of being the only North American animal that can hang by its tail.

Having survived for some three and a half months, the offspring must soon fend for themselves since it will not be long before their mother produces her second, annual litter. While insects comprise a substantial proportion of the opossum's diet, the creature is sufficiently omnivorous to devour just about anything from creepy crawlies to carrion.

Once a young opossum is on its own, one wonders how a creature whose brain is one sixth the size of a raccoon's manages to survive in the wild for even the brief 3-4 years normally allotted by Nature. Fortunately, there are several reasons for the successful survival of this species. In addition to producing large families twice a year, the opossum has 50 sharp teeth, more than any other North American mammal, that bite most effectively. Moreover, the creature is secretive and nocturnal, a superb climber, and possesses a fine sense of smell that is invaluable in finding food.

When threatened by another wild creature, the opossum shrieks, bares its impressive dental endowment in a most menacing manner and, in terms of rear-guard action, expels a foulsmelling substance that many predators find quite repulsive. Should a predator persist, however, the opossum's last-ditch defense is a superb performance of the act that has made the marsupial famous: playing 'possum. For several minutes, or for several hours if need be, the opossum tries to convince the enemy that it has suddenly become a most unappetizing corpse. Should the performance be sufficiently convincing, the opossum eventually gets up and goes on its way.

CHAPTER 17.

NEVER TOO OLD TO PLAY
(Florida River Otter)

People who have had extensive experience with otters invariably find them to be highly intelligent, friendly, and fascinating creatures. Although otters lead an extremely active life, and thus require a great deal of food, their remarkable aquatic ability enables them to expend minimal effort in order to satisfy their appetites. Thus, unlike so many wild animals, otters have plenty of free time in which to socialize and play.

While otters once flourished throughout this country, with the exception of extremely arid regions, their population is now considerably reduced and largely confined to the eastern seaboard states and those along the shores of the Gulf of Mexico. Generations of trappers have prized their pelts, many waters that once harbored their prey are now polluted, and development continues to encroach upon the creatures' natural habitats.

Fortunately, the Florida River Otter thrives in the maze of canals created by Lee County Mosquito Control. However, one is most likely to see otters in "Ding" Darling, particularly on the left side of Wildlife Drive. The sleek, streamlined animal is so beautifully adapted for swimming smoothly and effortlessly that it is not easy to detect a telltale wake in those brackish waters. Therefore, one should look for this supremely aquatic creature along the shores, where it often likes to consume freshly caught prey, slide in the mud, and socialize with other otters.

A typical otter is about 4' long, weighs around 20 pounds, and boasts a shiny coat of brown, waterproof fur. While otters move rather clumsily on land, they are extraordinarily graceful under water, be it fresh, brackish, or salty. Their webbed feet provide considerable propulsion which, accompanied by rippling undulations of strong body muscles and steering provided by a powerful tail, enable the creatures to swim with considerable speed. According to Sanibel naturalist George Campbell, an otter can outswim an alligator!

Given its enviable aquatic ability, the otter is not obliged to devote a great deal of time to finding food. While fishermen often dislike otters, it appears that the fish-eating mammal is really not at all partial to game fish. It does, however, have a great passion for crayfish and is quite happy to include snakes, frogs, turtles and crabs in its daily diet. Whatever the prey, it is quickly disposed of by a snap of the otter's powerful jaws and the slashing and tearing of its sharp teeth.

Several years ago, a Captiva winter resident had a unique experience with an orphaned otter that was merely 8″ long. For about five months, her secluded pond provided a safe haven for the defenseless creature that she sought to save from imminent extinction (courtesy of cars, dogs, alligators, etc.) and return to the wild once it was able to fend for itself. Since the otter is such a friendly animal, it was extremely difficult to avoid human "imprinting" that might well render it incapable of surviving in the wild. Fortunately, the orphaned otter was privileged to spend her childhood in the pond of Laura Riley, a wildlife photographer of national renown and a staunch supporter of CROW. Mrs. Riley's observations provide a rare and wholly reliable insight into the life style of an otter, and I am deeply indebted to her for sending me a wonderfully detailed and beautifully written account.

Like all those who have come into close contact with otters, Laura Riley was enchanted by the creature's playful nature, but had to steel herself to avoid potentially fatal imprinting. A ping pong ball tossed into the pond to encourage "Jenny" to explore deeper waters became a favorite toy, and Mrs. Riley subsequently discovered that the otter had taken to collecting shells that it found in the pond. Indeed, the creature's manual dexterity was particularly impressive when it carefully examined rocks, leaves and nuts.

Laura Riley also had the unique opportunity to observe the otter in its most natural habitat, under water. There, otters are able to "hurtle along like subsurface guided missiles" at 6-7 MPH. Moreover, Jenny could remain submerged for about five minutes, and stop to walk on the bottom in order to examine something that caught her interest.

Although Jenny did not survive very long after she was restored to the wild, one may derive some comfort from the knowledge that she died of natural, Darwinian causes — and not from speeding cars. Moreover, had it not been for the concern and care of Laura Riley, the 8″ orphan would probably not have survived long enough to enjoy any life at all.

CHAPTER 18.

GATOR AID
(American Alligator)

Although the gaping maw, sharp teeth and powerful jaws of the armor-plated alligator render it a terrifying beast to behold, many people are extremely eager to see this descendant of prehistoric behemoths. Thus in view of the potential danger posed by the wrong kind of contact between *Alligator mississippiensis* and *Homo sapiens*, the latter will want to be aware of certain facts concerning the former.

First and foremost, IT IS ILLEGAL TO FEED ALLIGATORS IN FLORIDA. Since the ancient reptile is endowed with a brain that is no bigger than a Bing cherry, the creature is quite incapable of distinguishing between the human hand that feeds it and whatever that hand happens to hold. Moreover, alligators that come to expect human handouts may lose all fear of Man and become dangerous "nuisance alligators."

One should also be aware of the fact that several hundred pounds of primordial instincts that are primarily programmed for sustenance, snoozing and sex should *never* be disturbed in any way. Do not be deceived by the creature's slow, clumsy waddle on land. When sufficiently inspired or irritated, an alligator can quickly go into overdrive and lunge at the source of its interest or annoyance.

Although an alligator is *potentially* dangerous to anyone who fails to observe the two, sensible commandments (Thou shalt not feed and Thou shalt not disturb), Man has little to fear from an enormous reptile that is really not the least bit interested in him. Thus Islanders and many winter residents have an affectionate regard for alligators, are often immensely proud of their particular resident reptile, give it a name, and become quite concerned when it fails to appear.

Indeed, most Islanders and "Snowbirds" love to tell alligator stories. For many years, a couple that vacationed in the pink cottages of *By the Sea* insisted upon renting an undersirable unit right off Gulf Drive rather than one closer to the beach; they loved to watch an enormous alligator that was particularly partial to the roadside ditch and frequently sunned in their back yard. Moreover, winter residents at the nearby *High Tide* cottages recall a memorable cocktail hour by the beach when someone calmly announced, "I believe we're about to be joined by an alligator," whereupon the group dispersed with dispatch (but not panic), and subsequently resumed preprandial libations shortly after the alligator had passed through their impromptu lounge.

Oddly enough, the affectionate regard for these reptiles on Sanibel includes even "nuisance alligators," like the legendary Marshall. In the fall of 1984, both island newspapers were deeply grieved to report the demise of the 12′ alligator weighing over 400 pounds which, for many of its 40-odd years, had been a real menace as king of the domain between Island Inn and Tarpon Bay Roads. Marshall, who may have been named for his predilection for marshmallows, became both a nuisance and a menace because people could not resist feeding him, with the result that he lost all fear of Man.

Marshall performed a great service by killing younger male alligators that attempted to invade his territory, thereby preventing a population explosion of gators in his kingdom. Moreover, not all the stories about his antics are apocryphal. The creature occasionally halted traffic on Tarpon Bay Road, and did indeed do battle with a Trans Am to the extent of bashing in the car's rear fender with his powerful tail, thereby causing the terrified driver to run his car into a ditch.

The "Ding" Darling Wildlife Refuge is definitely the best place to observe alligators from a safe distance, especially along the banks to the left of Wildlife Drive. A covey of cars parked at the side of the road frequently indicates that people are watching an alligator snoozing in the sun, or staring in horrified fascination as a splendid specimen submerges for a few moments, then suddenly emerges to capture a careless bird with a definitive snap of its powerful jaws.

The sight of an alligator making a meal out of a beautiful bird is just the kind of dastardly deed that one expects from a prehistoric creature whose ancestors roamed the earth well over 100 million years ago. Indeed, the alligator is not at all finicky about food and will gladly devour many mammals, birds, fish, reptiles, crustaceans and insects that have the misfortune to be in the wrong place at the right time, so far as one of the world's largest living reptiles is concerned.

In fact, however, the alligator's rather indiscriminate eating habits perform an important role in terms of preventing the overpopulation of many species and promoting the survival of the fittest. Thus many birds survive infancy thanks to the fact that alligators patrol nesting areas and strongly discourage incursions by a number of dangerous predators, particularly those capable of climbing trees.

As indicated in Chapter 2, alligators perform yet another vital function that is crucial to the survival of all mannner of wildlife. During the dry season, they dig below the water table in order to create a pond in which to immerse their bodies and keep their skin moist. Were it not for such sources of fresh water during a drought, many species of wildlife would perish. Thus one can hardly blame an alligator for consuming creatures that linger too long at its spa!

While a relatively mature alligator is clearly built for survival, its hapless offspring are tasty treats for a vast array of predators. Thus in order to ensure the survival of the species, Nature has endowed the female with the ability to lay some 30-50 eggs after mating with the male, a seemingly awkward procedure between behemoths that begins with a great deal of "come hither" bellowing by the male. Once hatched, the miniature alligators grow about one foot a year for a number of years *if* they manage to escape the attention of raccoons, turtles, otters, certain birds, *etc.*

Alas, Nature can do nothing about Man's craving for alligator purses, belts, shoes and wallets, with the result that the ancient reptile is currently listed by the federal government as a threatened species. Fortunately, *Alligator mississippiensis* will always find a safe haven on Sanibel.

CHAPTER 19.

INTRODUCTION

Ardent birders are extraordinarily patient people. They will climb mountains, tramp for miles over all manner of terrain in every kind of weather, and brave biting bugs while bushwhacking through mangrove swamps. In short, human hardship and extreme discomfort rarely deter a determined birder, for training powerful binoculars on a lofty nest or catching a glimpse of a splendid soaring specimen are the kinds of ineffable experiences that dedicated birders find so richly rewarding.

I once knew an ardent birder who made the supreme sacrifice in order to add a particular species to his "life list." He agreed to accompany his wife (and her 17 suitcases) to Europe if she would consent to spend some time in the Swiss mountains. Although totally exhausted upon his return, Osborne was elated to report that he had sighted an Alpine Chough (rhymes with rough).

Many people come to Sanibel in order to see birds, and those who visit during the winter months are especially fortunate in being able to observe about 150 resident and migratory species. Since the latter established a winter residence on this barrier island long before Man discovered and developed it, they are indeed our original "Snowbirds." Moreover, the sight of a pink cloud of Roseate Spoonbills flying in to feed at "Ding" Darling will surely convince anyone that migrating birds are among Sanibel's star avian attractions.

While experienced birders can identify a distant specimen from its silhouette, budding birdwatchers are often discouraged by the fact that the silhouette of a bird in flight is entirely different from that of the same species perched on a branch. Indeed, the identification of birds poses a number of problems for amateurs for, unlike stationary plants, birds have a highly disconcerting habit of flitting about willy-nilly. Thus it is easy to lose sight of them while fiddling around with the focusing mechanism on one's binoculars.

Moreover, amateur birders seeking to identify birds from the color of their feathers soon find that a number of species seem determined to defy identification. Thus the coloration of a particular bird may vary considerably depending on whether it is male or female, immature or adult. As an additional fillip, some species display special plumage during the breeding season!

Fortunately, so far as novice naturalists are concerned, many of Sanibel's most popular and beautiful birds are not at all difficult to identify. Moreover, their feeding habits are of considerable interest to all observers, be they expert or novice bird watchers. Photographs of all avian species discussed in the following chapters appear in the color section of this book.

CHAPTER 20.

HERONS

I once spent an entire afternoon trying to find out precisely what ornithologists mean when they say that a particular bird is a heron, a task that was considerably complicated by the fact that so *many* birds are called herons, true herons, white herons, very close relatives of herons, *etc.* According to the *Encyclopaedia Britannica*, a heron is simply "any long-legged, long-necked wading bird of the suborder Ardeae, order Ciconiiformes." Alas, there are times when that incredible compendium of human knowledge confuses far more than it clarifies in the eyes of amateur naturalists!

Fortunately, many people still have some dim recollection of chanting "kingdom, phylum, class, order, family, genus and species" in a high-school biology class. Thus if one refuses to be intimidated by the *Britannica's* reference to order and suborder and concentrates on family, one finds that there are indeed several families of herons. One includes the "true" herons discussed in this chapter, and another includes the White Ibis and the Roseate Spoonbill described in subsequent chapters.

Since the several families of herons comprise some 30 genera and about 60 species throughout the world, one begins to understand why ornithologists call so many different birds herons. In the final analysis, they are indeed wading birds with long legs, long necks, and long bills.

GREAT BLUE HERON

Although the suffix "ish" is generally applied to the coloration of the huge heron with the yellowish beak, whitish head and neck, and generally grayish-blue appearance elsewhere (with the exception of flesh-colored legs), even a totally novice bird-watcher is home free when it comes to identifying what is undoubtedly Sanibel's tallest bird. The creature can stretch to a height of 4', thanks primarily to the combined length of its legs, neck and beak. Moreover, its wingspan is about 6'.

The Great Blue Heron is indeed a wading bird that is fully capable of stalking its prey in shallow waters, be they fresh or salty. However, with apologies to the poet, John Milton, the creature is not unaware of the fact that they are also served who only stand and wait. Thus one commonly sees the big bird standing quite motionless with its head all hunched up on its shoulders, waiting with the patience of Job for something to swim, slither, or crawl within its reach. When it does, the Great Blue Heron may either spear the prey or else use its bill like a pair of scissors. Given such versatility, the big bird is able to capture fish, frogs, snakes, mice and even other birds with great dispatch.

LITTLE BLUE HERON

In discussing the Little Blue Heron, ornithologists invariably dwell upon two of its characteristics: one is quite confusing, while the other is rather amusing. So far as the former is concerned, considerable confusion is caused by the fact that this common wading bird comes in three different color combinations! In other words, an infant appears to be one species, an adolescent another, and only an adult really looks like a bird that one could call a Little Blue Heron.

Fortunately, a mature Little Blue Heron poses no problems in terms of identification, for it is considerably smaller than the Great Blue. Moreover, it has slaty-blue plumage, a warm brown head and neck, a bluish bill with a blue-black tip, and greenish legs. While the adult Little Blue does not sow confusion among the ranks of amateur birders, its infants and adolescents most certainly do!

The adolescent or immature Little Blue looks very much like an egret, especially a Snowy Egret. The two species are frequently confused because they are both about the same size, have pure-white plumage, and often go wading together in search of prey. However, the beak-legs-feet approach to identification should quickly clear up any confusion. Like adult Little Blues, the immature has the same greenish legs and bluish bill with the blue-black tip, whereas the legs and bill of the Snowy Egret are jet black and, of course, it boasts those telltale "golden slippers."

Unfortunately, infant Little Blue Herons pose considerable problems in terms of identification. In the late spring, one may see a year-old specimen in the process of molting in preparation for its adolescent white phase. At that time, the bird's plumage is blotched blue and white, or vice versa, and even an experienced birder may be tempted to add a new species to his "life list." However, the blotched bird that is sometimes called a "Calico Heron" is merely a Little Blue indulging in infantile disguise.

Having dealt with the three phases of the Little Blue's plumage, many authorities turn their attention to a rather delicate topic. It seems that some species of birds are strictly monogamous throughout their lives, others remain faithful for a single breeding season, and a few favor harems. Theoretically, the Little Blue falls into the second category. However, those who have observed Little Blues in their nesting areas invariably report that infidelity runs rampant in the rookery!

TRICOLORED HERON (LOUISIANA HERON)

Of the three species of blue herons described in this chapter, only the Tricolored's plumage is more blue than slaty blue, which leads one to wonder why it is the only one of the three that is not called some sort of blue heron. In any event, it is impossible to confuse the Tricolored with the Great Blue, for the latter is in a category all by itself in terms of size.

Although the Little Blue is about the same size as the Tricolored, the latter's white underparts readily distinguish it from the former. Even the underside of the Tricolored's neck is white, blotched with blue. Finally, for the benefit of those who catch a rear view of the bird, the creature has a white patch on its back.

One of Sanibel's most common herons, the Tricolored is an extremely active feeder. While it wades in shallow water like its relatives, the Tricolored often breaks into a run in order to pursue passing prey. Moreover, unlike most herons, the Tricolored does not confine its fishing forays to shallow waters. At times, it wades out into deeper water as though preparing to take a refreshing swim. However, since the bird is not able to swim, its purpose is probably to catch larger fish that may not venture into shallow waters.

The mention of larger prey brings up an interesting point. Like many herons, the Tricolored seems to be convinced that there is no such thing as biting off more than one can chew or, in this case, swallow. Griffing Bancroft once spent a quarter of an hour observing a spirited struggle between a Tricolored and a snake that it had stabbed with its customary, incredible speed. Although the prey was half as long as the predator, the heron managed to swallow most of the snake and fly off with the victim's tail dangling from its bill, doubtless awaiting the digestion of the head.

The remarkable speed and effectiveness of the Tricolored's stiletto-like bill generally ensures not only a steady supply of food but also the survival of the species. Although the bird may look like an innocuous question mark when standing on its nest, an avian intruder seeking to snatch an egg suddenly realizes that such a question mark is a deadly form of punctuation. More often than not, the predator never lives long enough to learn a lesson from such knowledge.

CHAPTER 21.

WHITE IBIS

As indicated in the introduction to this section, bird identification is frequently complicated by the fact that the color of a creature's plumage may change considerably between immaturity and adulthood. The body of the mature Ibis is as white as the driven snow, with the exception of a splash of black on the tips of its wings that is not very visible unless the bird is in flight. However, the plumage of the bird's immature offspring is brownish on top and white underneath for about two years!

Fortunately, an amateur birder is spared the embarrassment of including both the mature and the immature specimens as different species in his "life list" by virtue of the fact that *all* White Ibises have a long and most distinctive reddish beak that curves downward. Moreover, regardless of age, the bird's face, legs and feet are also rather red. Although all the reddish portions of the adult White Ibis turn to a flaming red during the breeding season, that relatively minor transformation poses no problems in terms of identifying the bird when it is in the throes of passion.

Since the long-legged White Ibis is a wading bird, entire flocks feed every day in the shallow waters of "Ding" Darling. Once again, the structure of this water bird's bill dictates the precise manner in which it feeds. The long, curved bill of the White Ibis is ideally suited for poking around in the mud, invading the hiding holes of various crustaceans, soft mollusks, *etc.*, and subsequently bringing to the surface all manner of tasty marine morsels.

Herons and egrets commonly accompany the White Ibis as it probes for hidden delicacies. Since their bills are not designed to poke, prod and dislodge, they "tailgate" in the hope of seizing the prey of the White Ibis before the latter has a chance to consume it!

When the White Ibis has had its fill of feeding and fending off piratical birds, it heads for home around sunset. In this area, home is generally a small mangrove island in Pine Island Sound or San Carlos Bay. Boaters who return to their docks at that time are frequently rewarded by the sight of the synchronized soaring and flying of a large flock of White Ibises. While "tailgating" herons, egrets, *et al.* often head for the same rookery, there always seems to be room at the small island inn.

Unlike the Great Egret, the White Ibis was not hunted by Man for its plumage. However, the bird found favor with the Indians as a source of food, and subsequent settlers hunted the creature for the same reason. According to Griffing Bancroft, early Floridians frequently featured the White Ibis as the main course for Thanksgiving and Christmas dinners! Fortunately, the bird is now fully protected under the law, and many generations of Sanibel visitors will be able to enjoy the sight of the snowy white wading bird with the strangely curved, red beak.

CHAPTER 22.

ROSEATE SPOONBILL

Although there are six species of spoonbills in the world, only the Roseate boasts bright, pink plumage. Moreover, much to our great good fortune, it happens to be the only spoonbill found in the United States. Despite its spatulate bill and bald head, the bird's magnificent pink plumage more than compensates for attributes that some might consider to be unaesthetic aberrations.

Alas, Man often covets beautiful feathers, with the result that beauty may prove to be not only the bane of a bird's existence but the cause of its extinction. As indicated in the next chapter, plume hunters once threatened the survival of the Snowy and the Great Egrets. Needless to say, the highly colorful plumage of the Roseate Spoonbill did not escape the hunters' avid attention, for the bird's wings made splendid fans for wealthy ladies of leisure. Although such barbaric practices are no longer permitted in this country, the Roseate Spoonbills in some parts of the world were virtually exterminated, hapless victims of a fashionable fad.

Fortunately, Sanibel's vast "Ding" Darling sanctuary attracts large flocks of Roseate Spoonbills, and the best time to see them is early in the morning or late in the afternoon when they fly into the refuge. After pausing to rest and preen, the birds wade in the shallow waters and swing their spatulate beaks from side to side in the rhythmical manner of a metronome set at a fairly slow speed. Special nerve ends run down the length of the bird's beak and, when the wide tip makes contact with a tasty treat, the bird instantly snaps it up.

While the pelican is definitely Sanibel's top tourist attraction among avian species, and appears in one form or another on all manner of merchandise, it cannot hold a candle to the spoonbill in terms of sheer beauty. Thus the Roseate Spoonbill, and not the Brown Pelican, has a very special place in the hearts of both Islanders and winter residents.

Not so very long ago, Sanibel was largely an undeveloped spit of sand that boasted little more than simple clusters of cottages along the Gulf of Mexico by way of accommodations. Devoted winter residents came year after year and stayed for several months at the small cottage colonies of *By the Sea, High Tide, Sanibel Cottages, etc.* Each colony had its own particular customs and traditions and, for many years, one of the most cherished traditions of the winter residents at *High Tide* was observing the return of the Roseate Spoonbills.

Since Roseate Spoonbills never return to "Ding" Darling on a given day at the end of February, about a dozen "Snowbirds" from *High Tide* used to park their cars by the observation tower on Wildlife Drive in the late afternoons for some ten days or more. During that period of time, they enjoyed modest preprandial libations with hors d'oeuvres and shared both of the preceding with any visitor who stopped to inquire about what the group was waiting to see.

The sociable vigil continued until someone finally sighted a pink cloud in the distance. As the cloud approached, it soon became clear that a large flock of Roseate Spoonbills had not forgotten their winter sanctuary at "Ding" Darling and its abundance of succulent marine morsels. The spoonbills invariably descended on their way to the tiny mangrove islands to the left of the observation tower, and the silent Snowbirds of *High Tide* marveled at the spectacular shades of pink against the dramatic background of a setting sun.

Such an ineffable sight elicited neither loud cheers nor raucous celebration. Rather, *High Tide's* winter residents felt humbly grateful for the return of what they considered to be the most beautiful "Snowbird" on Sanibel. Although the old cottages of *High Tide, et al.,* have now been replaced by condominium complexes bearing the same names, the Roseate Spoonbills have not changed at all. They still return to Sanibel every year, and are a thing of beauty in the eye of every beholder.

CHAPTER 23.

EGRETS

Many authorities call egrets white herons, for they are indeed herons. The three species of egrets that one is most likely to see on Sanibel all have white plumage and, to add to the confusion, the Little Blue Heron goes through a white phase, and we also have many White Ibises! Since the amateur birder will certainly see all five of the above, identification by plumage is clearly out of the question. Thus whenever you see a white bird on Sanibel, forget about feathers and take a closer look at its beak, legs and feet. While the beak-legs-feet approach to the identification of such beautiful birds seems almost sinful, it is certainly very sensible.

GREAT EGRET

Although the Great Egret is the largest of the three species of egrets that one commonly sees on Sanibel, small, larger and largest are purely relative terms for the benefit of the initiated. However, a big white bird with a yellow beak and coal-black legs and feet is definitely a Great Egret. During the breeding season, the adults develop a tuft of long, silky plumes on their backs. Unfortunately, those magnificent "nuptial plumes" almost caused the extinction of the species, courtesy of avid plume hunters.

Since the Great Egret is a wading bird, one can count on seeing it in the shallow waters of "Ding" Darling. There is nothing at all frenetic about the feeding habits of the big, white bird as it stalks its prey with very due, deliberate speed. However, since variety is supposed to be the spice of life, the Great Egret may occasionally forsake tedious wading in mucky waters in favor of stalking on *terra firma.* Perhaps a little lizard, or some other manageable land animal, will be its reward for such a show of initiative.

Like so many of Sanibel's water birds, entire colonies of Great Egrets nest in the small mangrove islands of San Carlos Bay and Pine Island Sound, rookeries that are virtually teeming with all manner of avian life. Although the males of some species are monogamous throughout life, others plight their troth for a single breeding season, several cheat on their mates, and a few favor small harems. On the whole, female birds whose male counterparts are not inordinately endowed with flashy feathers receive the greatest support from their mates after fertilization, during incubation, and until such time as their offspring are able to fend for themselves.

The male Great Egret is a splendid example of a *pater familias.* Throughout what must be an exceedingly boring period of incubation, he frequently spells his mate by performing what scientists refer to as "nest relief." Just prior to relieving the female at the nest, the male raises his wings and nuptial plumes and caresses his mate with his head. The female responds with a similar display of affection, and flies off to enjoy a period of freedom.

SNOWY EGRET

Although the Snowy Egret is much smaller and far more active than the Great Egret, such general observations are of little help to amateurs in distinguishing between the several species of white birds that one sees on Sanibel. Armed with the prosaic beak-legs-feet approach to identification, however, anyone who sees a white wading bird with a black beak, black legs, and bright yellow feet will immediately know that he has sighted a Snowy Egret. Of course, the "golden slippers" that are the bird's most distinctive feature may not always be visible when the creature is wading.

However, no one can fail to recognize a Snowy Egret during the breeding season, when extraordinarily fine nuptial plumes adorn the bird's back and breast and crown its head. Alas, not so very long ago, the pride of the Snowy Egret nearly caused its extinction when western milliners decided that a hat festooned with such splendid plumes would indeed be a thing of beauty and a joy forever. Moreover, those same nuptial plumes were also highly prized in the Orient, where they were used to decorate ceremonial robes.

144

It was not long before the egrets' breeding plumes were worth far more than their weight in gold, a fashion phenomenon that inspired plume hunters to invade rookeries during the breeding season when the plumes were in their full glory, and when the nesting birds were most vulnerable. Since the long, nuptial plumes of the Snowy Egret were even more silky and lacy than those of the Great Egret, the former was a particularly prime target.

However, shotgun blasts killed both species willy-nilly, other species in the rookeries as well, and caused birds to flee from their nests. Thus countless eggs never hatched because the parents had either been killed or frightened away. Fortunately, fashion is fickle, the fad passed, and the law now protects birds from plume hunters.

In general, the main purpose of nuptial plumes is to erect them and display their full glory for the benefit and admiration of a potential mate. However, since the Snowy Egret is quite a feisty bird, it frequently raises its nuptial plumes in order to scare off birds that presume to poach upon its self-assigned feeding territory.

As indicated at the beginning of this section, the Snowy Egret is far more active than the Great Egret. Indeed, the feeding habits of the former seem quite frenetic when compared to the slow, patient stalking of the latter. The Snowy Egret dashes through the water in order to scare and stir up small marine life that it subsequently captures in its beak with dart-like speed. Thus any tailgating bird that hopes to benefit from the labor of "golden slippers" is bound to be sorely disappointed.

CATTLE EGRET

The Cattle Egret has a yellow beak, dark legs and feet, and both its bill and neck are shorter and thicker than those of other herons. Since amateur birders are generally not that familiar with the length and width of the beaks and necks of herons, however, the very thought of identifying yet another white bird on

Sanibel that is just a bit smaller than the Snowy Egret may seem to be an impossible challenge.

Fortunately, one is rarely placed in the position of having to distinguish between a Cattle Egret and a number of other species of white herons for the simple reason that the former generally eschews the company of the latter. While the Cattle Egret is quite capable of wading in shallow water and feeding on marine morsels in the manner of its relatives, it prefers not to get its feet wet. Thus on Sanibel, one is most likely to see this interesting creature at the side of a road, in a vacant lot, or on a golf course where it hunts insects and little lizards.

Although the Cattle Egret is not usually found in the company of other herons and water birds, it becomes far more sociable during the breeding season. At that time, the bird develops orange-brown feathers on its back, breast, and on the crest of its head. Its yellow bill turns to a startling shade of purple, and only then does the Cattle Egret deign to join other avian species to breed and nest in the rookeries.

The Cattle Egret is actually an African immigrant that has made its way to many parts of the world. In the 1930s, strong tail winds may have enabled some of this species to fly across the Atlantic Ocean to South America. By the 1950s, Cattle Egrets were common in Florida, and they have subsequently extended their range as far north as Canada.

Since the bird is so partial to insects, it derived its name from the fact that it frequently follows cattle in the hope that the animals' hooves will churn up the soil and expose all manner of tasty treats. While we do not have herds of cattle on Sanibel, the adaptable Cattle Egret considers bulldozers and lawn mowers to be most acceptable substitutes!

CHAPTER 24.

ANHINGA

Anyone who looks up Anhinga in the dictionary will probably be told to see Darter, while the venerable *Encyclopaedia Britannica* orders seekers of Darter to see Snakebird. Moreover, some authoritative sources refuse to suggest that one "see" anything at all, thereby reserving enlightenment for those who already know that Water Turkey is yet another common name for the Anhinga!

In any event, all three nicknames aptly describe several common characteristics of the swimming and diving Anhingas of tropical and subtropical America. They are called Darters because they seem to dart around in the water, or Snakebirds since only the neck and head are visible when they swim, or Water Turkeys in view of their rather long, turkey-like tail.

Oddly enough, the common names do not refer to what is probably the most distinguishing characteristic of the Anhinga: its neck. Although the first seven vertebrae form a concave curve, the eighth is nearly at right angles to the seventh, the ninth suddenly swoops downward, and the remaining vertebrae form a convex curve! However, such vertebral vagaries apparently endow the Anhinga with an extraordinary degree of flexibility, with the result that the bird is peerless when it comes to spearfishing. In fact, its dagger-like bill often penetrates fish so effectively that the Anhinga must swim to shore and dislodge its impaled prey in order to consume it.

Unlike most water birds, the Anhinga is not equipped with special oil glands that keep its feathers relatively waterproof when it dives and swims. Thus the bird must frequently perch and spread its wings in order to dry out before embarking upon the next fishing foray, a common sight at the "Ding" Darling Refuge.

Since Cormorants are black birds of the same order that also spread out their wings for the same reason, they are often mistaken for Anhingas. However, the former lack the telltale neck of the latter, and an adult Anhinga has white patches on its wings and tail in addition to a white line on its neck. Moreover, a Cormorant swims with its body *above* the water, and grabs fish with its hooked beak.

147

CHAPTER 25.

CORMORANT

The word cormorant usually refers to the large, black-feathered diving birds with hooked beaks and webbed feet that are found throughout the world, the Double-Crested Cormorant being the specimen that one sees on Sanibel, often spreading its wings to dry in the manner of Anhingas. Although cormorant is also defined as a gluttonous person, that fact is not commonly known. Thus one may insult with impunity someone who eats like a pig by remarking that he eats like a Cormorant, and the glutton will probably bless you for saying that he eats like a bird!

The voracious appetites of Cormorants, coupled with their swimming and diving abilities, have not escaped the attention of mankind. For many centuries, Man has tamed and trained Cormorants to do their fishing for them! Thus the Master of the Cormorants was once a valued member of the royal household in England. While Cormorant fishing is no longer prevalent in Europe, it remains a time-honored tradition in the Orient.

China is generally cited as the prime example of an Oriental country in which Cormorant fishing has been practiced since time immemorial. However, I chanced to come across a book by Frederic de Garis entitled *Their Japan* (Yokohama, 1936), in which the author described in fascinating detail all manner of Japanese traditions and customs, including Cormorant fishing. I am deeply indebted to M. de Garis for the following summary of the hereditary occupation of Cormorant fishing for over 1,000 years in the town of Gifu on the banks of the Nagara River. As readers will soon note, either the author or the Japanese fishermen had an obsession with the number twelve.

Early in the evening, 12 boats would set forth on the Nagara River a few miles upstream from Gifu and slowly drift down to that town for several hours. Each boat was equipped with a mass of blazing pine knots in a cage suspended from the bow in order to attract the fish, and each boat contained 12 Cormorants. The birds had been captured as infants and easily tamed and trained for a year or two. Now, they waited to respond to the command of the lead fisherman, who controlled them by means of 12 cords of spruce fiber about 12' long to which each bird was attached. Moreover, lest the birds devour the small *Ayu* fish that they subsequently caught, a ring of cord around their necks precluded that possibility.

Once set in the water, the Cormorants darted around and fished with voracious vigor while the head fisherman skillfully avoided entanglements among the 12 lines of his master cord. Whenever he spied a bird with an extremely distended throat, indicating the tightly packed presence of perhaps half a dozen *Ayu*, he gently hauled in the Cormorant, tipped it upside down and, despite vigorous protests, obliged the bird to disgorge its prey into a large basket.

Since the 12 birds caught about 450 *Ayu* apiece during several hours of fishing, one boat could count on over 5,000 small fish, and the combined catch of all 12 boats in the flotilla would be well over 60,000 *Ayu!* M. de Garis' calculations did not include the possibility of sinking to the bottom of the Nagara River under the sheer weight of *Ayu* fish. Finally, after several hours of frustrating fishing from the Cormorants' point of view, the birds were allowed to gorge like gluttons. Not surprisingly, a Cormorant could fish for Man for about 12 years.

As indicated in the preceding chapter, the Double-Crested Cormorant looks a great deal like an Anhinga and both birds have very similar habits. On Sanibel, one occasionally sees a Cormorant (but not an Anhinga) staggering around in a totally disoriented manner as though it were drugged or drunk. There is some speculation that the bird may have consumed contaminated fish, possibly victims of a Red Tide. Should you ever see such a helpless Cormorant, call CROW immediately (472-3644). That fine organization has had considerable success in nursing disoriented Cormorants back to health and restoring them to the wild.

CHAPTER 26.

BLACK SKIMMER

Most people are far more interested in a bird's lovely plumage than in its utilitarian beak. However, since the latter frequently determines the manner in which the creature captures its prey, the feeding habits of Sanibel's water birds are especially fascinating to observe.

The Anhinga dives under water and impales prey on its sharply pointed beak; the equally aquatic Cormorant grabs fish firmly at either end with its hooked beak; and the long, curved bill of the Ibis is ideal for poking around for a meal in shallow waters. However, as if to remind us that beaks are by no means the *sine qua non* in terms of feeding, Ospreys fish with their feet!

The long-legged sea bird known as the Black Skimmer is both a beautiful bird and a miracle of avian engineering. Its lower bill, which is extremely thin and considerably longer than its upper bill, actually skims the water and scoops up fish while the creature continues to fly just a few inches above the surface! Although such skimming may cause the bird to ingest a few insects, the Black Skimmer does not take in water or touch the surface with any other part of its body, for to do so would surely result in death by drowning.

The Black Skimmer prefers to feed at night, when fish are generally closer to the surface of calmer waters. Fortunately, the bird frequently goes fishing during the day as well, and one often sees the lovely creature skim the surface of the water, rise at the end of its run, turn around, and skim the same area. Since the Black Skimmer generally repeats this process several times, some authorities speculate that the little silvery wake produced by its skimming may lure fish to the surface, and to their fate.

Sanibel's summer visitors are often delighted to see scores of Black Skimmers nesting in the sand of extremely exposed areas. In the mid-1980s, a large colony of those birds used the Causeway islands as a nesting area for many weeks. While birdwatchers were elated to find a nesting area that, for once, was both readily accessible and highly visible, the benefits to birders and casual observers were far outweighed by the potential danger to the nesting birds in the eyes of many concerned individuals.

In an effort to prevent people from frightening the birds by coming too close to their nests, personnel from "Ding" Darling cordoned off the area with bright, orange ribbon. However, there was always the fear that adult Black Skimmers might become alarmed, flee from their nests, and leave the eggs exposed to both predators and the lethal rays of the subtropical sun.

While the incubation process of many species involves keeping eggs warm until they hatch, Black Skimmers must provide shade for their eggs lest they boil and die. Thus the Sanibel-Captiva Conservation Foundation placed 50 decoys in a secluded, sandy area early in the summer of 1984 in the hope that the birds would eschew the exposed Causeway spoil islands in favor of a private preserve on Sanibel. Unfortunately, the SCCF was not rewarded for its imaginative efforts in the summer of 1984. However, one can always hope that, in future years, the Black Skimmers may be more amenable, and the Conservation Foundation more successful.

CHAPTER 27.

OSPREY (FISH HAWK)

Since the Osprey has a white head, it is often mistaken for its famous hawk relative, the Bald Eagle. However, birders armed with binoculars will note the distinctive dark band across the Osprey's face, and its white breast is quite visible to the naked eye of more casual observers. When in doubt, it is fairly safe to assume that one has sighted an Osprey and not a Bald Eagle, for the latter rarely appears on Sanibel.

Oddly enough, hawks, eagles, vultures, owls and falcons have a great deal in common. They are carnivorous birds of prey equipped with strong, notched beaks, extemely sharp claws, and all are called raptors. Raptor is a word derived from a Latin verb meaning to seize and/or carry off, which is precisely what raptors do with their prey.

The Osprey plunges feet first into the water, often from a great height, in order to sink its sharp talons into a passing fish. Unfortunately, the fact that this raptor fishes with its feet is sometimes a fatal disadvantage. Should the impaled prey be too heavy for the bird to carry off, the sharp claws that usually ensure its survival may actually cause its death. Locked in a deadly embrace with its prey, the Osprey drowns as the heavy fish dives deeper into the water. Thus, from time to time, local fishermen reel in a big fish with only the claws of an ill-fated Osprey still clinging tenaciously to its prey.

Like other raptors, the Osprey is endowed with remarkable vision and can spot a potential meal from a distance of about two miles! Since such birds of prey must have a balanced diet in order to derive proper nourishment from delicacies like hair, fur and feathers, bones, and even insect parts, raptors hunt a variety of mammals, reptiles, birds and bugs. While Ospreys do not run the risk of being drowned by land animals, they are extremely vulnerable to pesticides that may have contaminated their prey. When DDT and other pesticides are absorbed by raptors, the birds subsequently produce eggs with extremely thin shells that break easily, thereby threatening the survival of the species.

It seems that the entire life style of the Osprey revolves around an addiction to height. It often dives from a considerable height in order to capture passing prey, and builds its nest in the tallest trees or utility poles. Unfortunately, as described in some detail at the end of Chapter 5, Ospreys are also addicted to collecting junk, and seepage from their nests sometimes produces pandemonium at the local power company. While the birds' predilection for utility poles is most regrettable, there is one pole on Sanibel that is adorned with a nest that appears to be both harmless and highly amusing. That particular pole is just outside the fire station on Palm Ridge Road. The speakers for the old fire alarm are mounted at the top of the pole, and an occupied Osprey nest is draped all over the speakers!

While no Osprey nest would ever be awarded the Good Housekeeping seal of approval, the birds seem to live in remarkable harmony amid all their clutter. Indeed, Nature has endowed the male Osprey with a charming characteristic that no female of any species could fail to appreciate. A Sanibel friend, who has observed Ospreys for many years, reports that although the male flies away from the female after mating, he soon returns and presents her with a fine fish. Surely no romantic novel could possibly provide its readers with a more inspiring example of continuing courtship and consideration following consummation.

CHAPTER 28.

BROWN PELICAN

Oddly enough, the Brown Pelican and the American Alligator have a great deal in common. Their respective ancestors inhabited the earth many millions of years ago, and neither creature has altered very much in its appearance over the millennia. Thus they both look quite prehistoric, which is a euphemistic way of saying that neither one would ever win a wildlife beauty contest! In the eyes of millions of visitors, however, the alligator and the pelican are Florida's leading wildlife attractions. While the former sends a shudder of fear down one's spine, the latter often provides comic relief.

Since the Brown Pelican looks like some prehistoric, flying reptile, it is impossible to confuse it with any other avian species on Sanibel. However, the expandable pouch below the lower beak, which can cope with over two gallons of water, should certainly resolve any doubts regarding the identity of the big gray bird with webbed feet that is the largest nesting bird in this area.

One might well wonder why an adult Brown Pelican that may live for over 20 years, and whose plumage is certainly far more gray than brown, should be named after immature progeny that are brown on top and white underneath. Alas, amateur birders are not privy to the arcana of ornithological nomenclature. However, anyone who spots a Brown Pelican with a tuft of bright yellow breeding plumage on the top of its head can impress his companions by remarking that the pelican will soon be in the throes of passion.

Fishing piers and marinas are certainly the best places to look for entire flocks of the big birds that have discovered the joys of human handouts. Although the sociable exchanges between fishermen and pelicans are frequently most rewarding from the latter's point of view, Man is often unaware of the fact that fish bones tossed in the direction of the voracious birds may tear their pouches, or that the creatures may become hopelessly entangled in monofilament fishing line. As a result, Brown Pelicans comprise the majority of CROW's avian patients.

In addition to seeing Brown Pelicans at fishing piers and marinas, no Sanibel visitor can fail to observe the creature soar 30' or more over the water, stall for a moment, then suddenly dive like a kamikaze pilot. While the seemingly clumsy crash landings may appear to be self-destructive rather than productive, Nature has endowed the bird with special air sacs to cushion the impact. Moreover, that very impact may serve to stun fish swimming near the surface, with the result that the Brown Pelican is generally able to scoop up its prey and, by tilting its head, get rid of a couple of gallons of salt water that would certainly prevent the bird from becoming airborne.

In 1910, at a time when clever limericks were highly fashionable, Dixon Lanier Merrick achieved a measure of immortality by inaccurately portraying the pelican as follows:

A wonderful bird is the pelican,
His bill will hold more than his belican.
He can take in his beak
Food enough for a week,
But I'm damned if I see how the helican.

While the pelican is indeed a wonderful bird, its bill cannot hold more than its belly can. In fact, the contents of the former could not begin to satisfy the hunger pangs of the latter for a single day, let alone an entire week. However, it is certainly true that the big Brown Pelican is a voracious eater, for it requires several pounds of fish a day in order to survive. Moreover, both male and female pelicans must try to cope with the seemingly insatiable appetites of their impatient progeny until the latter are able to fish for themselves.

The mangrove islands of San Carlos Bay and Pine Island Sound harbor substantial colonies of Brown Pelicans. While the adults are relatively quiet birds that eschew raucous squaking in favor of snapping their beaks when annoyed or alarmed, their offspring make a great deal of racket as they constantly clamor for food.

A newborn Brown Pelican has black skin, is completely naked, and only a mother could possibly love such an ugly offspring and put up with its constant demands for food. Although newborns are fed partially digested fish that the parent regurgitates, it is not long before the impatient young reach right into the adult's gullet as though it were a self-service cafeteria! Moreover, in their eagerness to grab goodies from the gullet, the young fight among themselves and swat each other over the head with their wings. Should the young become too obnoxious, the besieged adult may fly off for a few moments of precious peace.

Since there are hundreds of Brown Pelicans around Sanibel and Captiva, it is certainly hard to believe that the ancient bird claims the unenviable distinction of being listed as an endangered species by the federal government! In fact, however, the pelican population of several states, Louisiana in particular, dropped drastically until DDT was banned in the early 1970s.

Scientists surmised that pesticides containing DDT had contaminated the waters, thereby contaminating the small fish upon which the big bird preys. While DDT did not actually kill adult birds, the latter stored the poison in their systems and subsequently produced eggs with fatally fragile shells. Thus the eggs frequently broke when dropped in the nest, or were crushed under the weight of the incubating parent. Fortunately, the prehistoric bird that has survived for countless millennia is now on the road to recovery, and one hopes that future generations of Florida's visitors will continue to enjoy one of their favorite pastimes, pelican watching.

CHAPTER 29.

THE J.N. "DING" DARLING
NATIONAL WILDLIFE REFUGE

Despite discovery, subsequent development, and the presence of several hundred thousand annual visitors, there is every reason to believe that this tiny barrier island will always be unique. The salvation of Sanibel is primarily due to the Herculean efforts of a small group of island conservationists who were instrumental in protecting, *in perpetuity*, about half of this island from the mindless bulldozers and pile drivers of developers.

Although most members of that seemingly tireless and totally dedicated band of conservationists remain unsung heroes, their inspiring leader happened to be a nationally prominent Captiva winter resident, J.N. "Ding" Darling. Ding's widely syndicated and wonderfully satirical cartoons for the *Des Moines Register* earned him not only national renown but two Pulitzer prizes! Furthermore, the famous political cartoonist was also an ardent conservationist who carried considerable clout.

In 1934, President Roosevelt appointed Mr. Darling to head the U.S. Biological Survey, now called the U.S. Fish and Wildlife Service. In his official capacity, Ding bombarded the President with countless memoranda and poignant cartoons in an effort to secure federal funds for wildlife conservation, and Secretary of the Interior Ickes was constantly subjected to an even more relentless barrage. As a result of his efforts at the national level, Ding Darling was largely responsible for establishing the nation's network of game refuges and obtaining $17 million for the protection of wildlife. Not surprisingly, it was Ding who drew the first federal duck stamp.

In the late 1930s, Ding and his small group of island conservationists were determined to protect *all* wildlife on Sanibel. Although President Truman signed a proclamation in 1947 that declared this island to be a national wildlife refuge, that act was primarily designed to prohibit the killing or capturing of migratory birds and some mammals. It was clear to Ding and his conservationist friends that wildlife could never be adequately protected unless their natural habitats remained undisturbed.

Thus the group was instrumental in securing about 100 acres just off Tarpon Bay Road from the Bailey family. Unfortunately, Ding Darling died before the Bailey Tract finally came under the permanent protection of the U.S. Fish and Wildlife Service. Moreover, at the time of his death in 1962, the famous cartoonist and conservationist was doubtless aware of the fact that the Causeway would soon be completed, thereby inaugurating an era of rapid development that would most certainly threaten or destroy wildlife habitats on Sanibel.

Shortly after Ding Darling's death, his conservationist friends on the island felt compelled to complete his work. They formed the "Ding" Darling Memorial Committee and launched a vigorous campaign of cajoling, lobbying, endless meetings with various state and federal officials, and lengthy sessions with several private property owners. The final result of their heroic efforts is what we now call the J.N. "Ding" Darling National Wildlife Refuge, 4,900 acres of permanent wildlife sanctuary under the protection of the U.S. Fish and Wildlife Service. Moreover, the 100-acre Bailey Tract and a few more acres on Sanibel also enjoy the protection of that same federal agency.

Thanks to Ding Darling, and to the island conservationists who became so extraordinarily inspired by his leadership, all manner of wildlife will always find a safe haven on Sanibel. Every year, thousands of visitors enjoy the memorable experience of driving, biking, or hiking along the 5-mile loop known as Wildlife Drive in order to observe and photograph Nature's fascinating creatures in their natural habitats.

In addition to Wildlife Drive, the refuge has a fine new visitor's center where a series of exhibits portrays a variety of wildlife. Nature films are regularly featured in the auditorium, and both of Sanibel's local newspapers announce the refuge's program of films, "wet walks," *etc.* For further information about the refuge and all the programs that it offers to the public free of charge, call 472-1100.

CHAPTER 30.

THE SANIBEL-CAPTIVA CONSERVATION FOUNDATION

As indicated in the preceding chapter, the "Ding" Darling Memorial Committee deserves full credit for more than doubling the acreage under the protection of the former Sanibel National Wildlife Refuge established in the 1940s, with the result that the 4,900-acre bayside tract was renamed the J.N. "Ding" Darling National Wildlife Refuge in 1967. Although it certainly appeared that the Committee had achieved its goal of creating a suitable memorial for Ding Darling, it did not disband in 1967. On the contrary, most of its members, and a few new recruits, formed the Sanibel-Captiva Conservation Foundation in that very same year! This time, their primary goal was to save Sanibel's highly sensitive interior wetlands.

The island's 1,200 acres of fresh-water wetlands are the *sine qua non* in terms of attracting and sustaining our incredibly large variety of plant and animal life. Although other barrier islands once had such wetlands, they were drained and filled by developers. Thus on the very eve of massive development in the late 1960s, Sanibel was the only barrier island in Florida whose vital wetlands remained largely undisturbed. Unfortunately, merely 100 acres, the Bailey Tract, were protected.

The Sanibel-Captiva Conservation Foundation soon realized that outright purchase afforded the best and most permanent form of protection. Thus at the present time, about 850 acres are either owned or managed by the SCCF. While the purchase or protective management of Sanibel's interior wetlands remains a major goal of the Foundation, success in that endeavor at a highly critical time enabled the SCCF to concentrate on a number of corollary projects related to conservation. In that connection, education was very high on the list of priorities.

In 1978, the SCCF welcomed the public to its new Conservation Center. Situated on the Foundation's main, 207-acre tract, the energy-efficient building houses a variety of wildlife exhibits.

Many visitors enjoy the splendid display of shells that have made Sanibel famous, and the glassed-in area for live snakes, hissing, shedding their skins, or just snoozing. Other exhibits are devoted to the critical importance of fresh-water wetlands, the redeeming social value of alligators and, a most recent addition, the skull of the famous nuisance alligator, "Marshall."

The Foundation has opened ten nature trails on its main tract that visitors are invited to explore on their own, or join a one-hour tour conducted by a volunteer trail guide. During the season, a variety of films and lectures are presented at the Center, details of which are reported in both island newspapers. Moreover, the SCCF has published a series of interesting booklets about Sanibel's wildlife, ecology, *etc.*, several of which are listed in the brief bibliography at the end of this book.

In addition to its wide variety of educational endeavors, the Foundation has embarked upon a number of projects designed to protect wildlife and the environment in general. Since their efforts on behalf of Barn Owls, Ospreys, and Black Skimmers have been described in previous chapters, it is time to say a few words about a very major undertaking, the Native Plant Nursery.

Opened in 1979, the Nursery provides a convenient source of hardy native species for the landscaping purposes of both Islanders and developers. The Foundation strongly encourages the planting of native species rather than the more colorful exotics, for the cost of color is very high in terms of water and energy consumption. The Native Plant Nursery is under the direction of a qualified professional, one of the Foundation's few salaried staff members.

It seems almost miraculous that the SCCF should be able to undertake such a wide range of educational and environmental projects with a full-time staff of three people, and one is reminded of the delightful fairy tale about the elves who came out at night and performed a prodigious amount of work before disappearing at dawn. To the best of my knowledge, the Sanibel-Captiva Conservation Foundation does not harbor a host of hardworking elves in its building. However, the goals of the SCCF have succeeded in attracting the support of a small army of volunteers. Many are permanent residents, but even more are winter residents or "Snowbirds."

In 1980, the Foundation stated that its primary objective was "the mitigation of human impact on the natural ecosystem and environment so that the unique character of Sanibel and Captiva may be preserved for present and future generations." That is indeed a very tall order for a non-profit organization that receives neither state nor federal funds! However, many Islanders, "Snowbirds," and other visitors feel very strongly about preserving "the unique character of Sanibel and Captiva," with the result that several thousand people provide financial support, and scores of volunteers contribute their time as well.

Thus as early as 1972, volunteer woodsmen began to make the nature trails that are maintained by volunteers and along which other volunteers guide groups of visitors. A number of volunteers lend their time and talents to the office, the small gift shop, the Nursery, *etc.* For further information about the programs and goals of the Sanibel-Captiva Conservation Foundation, consult island newspapers, or call 472-2329.

CHAPTER 31.

CARE AND REHABILITATION OF WILDLIFE

Half of Sanibel can never be developed, thanks primarily to the "Ding" Darling Refuge and the Conservation Foundation, and wildlife is protected on both Sanibel and Captiva. Thus it comes as quite a shock to learn that wildlife remains at the mercy of mankind on these two sanctuary islands!

Sanibel, Captiva, and all of Florida have become increasingly popular vacation and retirement havens, with the result that man-caused injuries to wildlife multiply considerably every year. The loss of natural habitats due to development is but one of the many problems with which wildlife must cope and, as we have seen, only the raccoon and the Cattle Egret seem to find that development has redeeming features.

Unfortunately, the overwhelming majority of injuries sustained by wildlife are caused by Man's carelessness and general lack of awareness. Thus the pitiful roadside remains of raccoons, otters, opossums, armadillos, and many other species bear silent testimony to our failure to slow down and, on windy days, low-flying birds often become "Causeway casualties."

Quite unintentionally, fishermen are frequently responsible for injuring water birds, especially the endangered Brown Pelican. The latter will eagerly attempt to devour fish bones tossed to it out of friendly generosity, with the result that the sharp bones may tear its pouch. Moreover, pelicans and other birds often become hopelessly entangled in carelessly discarded monofilament fishing line.

Human beach litter can be fatal to a variety of avian species. The bright, circular tabs of soda pop cans often attract "pecking" birds, and their beaks may become clamped shut by those discarded metal objects. Moreover, one of the jettisoned plastic rings from a six-pack may become a noose around a bird's neck, with the result that the hapless creature cannot swallow its prey.

In the late 1960s, two island women rescued a pair of badly injured Royal Terns and brought those Causeway casualties to their home for care, rehabilitation, and subsequent restoration to the wild. Although they did not realize it at that time, Shirley Walter and Jessie Dugger had just become the founders of a unique organization for the Care and Rehabilitation of Wildlife that we now call CROW.

The founders' back-yard menagerie in a Sanibel subdivision grew by leaps and bounds. Shirley Walter picked up injured "critters" on the islands and from many parts of the mainland and, in two years, logged 80,000 miles on her car. Moreover, she regularly arose well before dawn and seined for fish in order to feed her growing number of wildlife patients. By 1972, CROW was duly incorporated as a non-profit organization, and Shirley Walter's annual report to the Florida Game and Fresh Water Fish Commission the following year stated that CROW had taken in 241 wildlife patients and succeeded in restoring 145 to the wild.

The achievements of CROW's founders were quite incredible, particularly in view of the fact that the care and rehabilitation of wildlife was a relatively virgin field that only a few pioneers were just beginning to explore. Quite understandably, however, residents of the Sanibel subdivision that housed CROW took a rather dim view of the matter when recuperating patients occasionally escaped the founders' back yard and romped on their roofs or splashed in their swimming pools. Thus after some seven years of heroic efforts on behalf of injured critters, CROW's founders realized that their back-yard hospital was desperately in need of a new home.

Fortunately, many people shared Shirley Walter's firm conviction that human beings have a moral obligation to help creatures that have suffered so severely from our presence. Thus for many years, a number of concerned Islanders and "Snowbirds" had provided CROW with financial support and, when that organization could no longer operate in a Sanibel subdivision, a Captiva winter resident offered her guest house and yard to CROW as a temporary haven.

The extraordinarily generous Captiva winter resident and savior of CROW was Adelaide "Jabber" Cherbonnier. While Jabber had offered to house CROW on a temporary basis until the organization was able to move to a permanent and more suitable location, and had also agreed to become CROW's president *pro tem*, her "temporary" housing and official tenure lasted for more than seven years!

Since Adelaide Cherbonnier was not always in residence, she immediately hired Holly Davies as Executive Director of CROW's Captiva hospital, a position that the latter continues to hold. Thus for some seven years, Jabber Cherbonnier had pelicans recuperating on her porch and raccoons under it, bags of unsavory specimens in her freezer awaiting shipment to the *Smithsonian*, and loons floating in the bathtub of her guest house.

Early in 1982, CROW finally moved to its permanent home off the Sanibel-Captiva Road, where a simple blue crescent marks the entrance. While the organization holds an occasional open house during the season, its premises are not normally open to the public at other times. Quite apart from the fact that CROW is primarily a hospital for injured wildlife and not a zoo, too much human contact with recuperating patients leads to a form of "imprinting" that would seriously impair their ability to survive when they are returned to the wild.

In view of the extremely delicate nature of its wildlife mission, CROW can never benefit from the kind of high visibility enjoyed by "Ding" Darling and the Conservation Foundation. Moreover, like the SCCF, CROW receives neither state nor federal funds and is thus entirely supported by contributions and occasional grants. Fortunately, many Islanders and Snowbirds are extremely generous contributors and volunteers.

Although CROW's salaried staff is presently limited to two, full-time employees, the organization cared for 688 injured critters of 113 different species in 1984 and was able to restore about one third of those patients to the wild! In many instances, the prompt action of volunteers spelled the difference between survival and extinction.

A number of volunteers transport injured wildlife to CROW from Sanibel, Captiva, and the mainland. Others have constructed a large, outdoor flight cage so that recuperating raptors can practice their flying and hunting skills before being released. Some volunteers help out in the office, and many are willing to cope with the dirty nitty-gritty of cleaning the patients' cages. For further information about Sanibel's lifeline for helpless wildlife, call CROW at 472-3644.

BRIEF BIBLIOGRAPHY

THE ENCYCLOPAEDIA BRITANNICA

In the beginning, there was the *Encyclopaedia*, immensely helpful in starting research on any subject. Articles are always authoritative, frequently exhaustive, and sometimes exhausting to read.

BOOKS AND ARTICLES

The following works are very readable and readily available on the islands.

Campbell, George, R. *The Nature of Things on Sanibel: A Discussion of the Animal & Plant Life of Sanibel Island with a Sidelong Glance at Some of Their Relatives Elsewhere.* Fort Myers, Florida: Press Printing Company, 1978.

Dormer, Elinore M. *The Sea Shell Islands: A History of Sanibel and Captiva.* Tallahassee, Florida: Rose Printing Company, 1979.

Greenberg, Margaret. "C.R.O.W.: The Care and Rehabilitation of Wildlife," *Island Life*, Volume 3, Number 1, Issue 7 (1984), 2-4.

Hall, Francis Wyly. *Palms and Flowers of Florida.* St. Petersburg, Florida: Great Outdoors Publishing Co., 1979.

Lendt, David L. *Ding: The Life of Jay Norwood Darling.* Ames, Iowa: Iowa State University Press, 1979.

Peterson, Lee. *A Field Guide to Edible Wild Plants of Eastern and Central North America.* Boston, Massachusetts: Houghton Mifflin Company, 1978.

Riley, Laura. "Jenny Who Makes the Day Begin," *Reader's Digest*, (March, 1982), 31-36.

Robbins, Chandler S., Bruun, Bertel, and Zim, Herbert S. *A Guide to Field Identification: Birds of North America.* New York: Golden Press, 1966.

Williams, Winston. *Florida's Fabulous Waterbirds: Their Stories.* Tampa, Florida: National Art Services, Inc., 1983.

Workman, Richard W. *Growing Native: Native Plants for Landscape Use in Coastal South Florida.* Sanibel, Florida: The Sanibel-Captiva Conservation Foundation, Inc., 1980.

BARRIER ISLAND NATURE PUBLICATIONS

The following booklets are published by the Sanibel-Captiva Conservation Foundation as part of its education program. Many of the authors are local naturalists whose careful studies and first-hand observations were of invaluable assistance in preparing *Nature on Sanibel.*

Bancroft, Griffing. *Roseate Spoonbills and Other Wading Birds of Sanibel-Captiva.* 1981.

Bancroft, Griffing and Tenney, George C. *Helping to Save Paradise: The Story of the Sanibel-Captiva Conservation Foundation.* 1981.

Campbell, George R. *Jaws, Too: The Story of Sanibel's Alligators and Other Crocodilians.* 1981.

Dormer, Elinore M. *The Calusa: Sanibel-Captiva's Native Indians.* 1981.

Harrison, Hal H. *Nesting Birds of Sanibel-Captiva and the Barrier Islands.* 1981.

Rhinesmith, Herbert S. *Water for Sanibel-Captiva.* 1982.

Shane, Emily. *Otters, Armadillos, Raccoons, Opossums.* 1982.

Sharma, Dinesh C. *Barrier Islands: Nature Vs. Man: How Sanibel and Captiva Fit into the Pattern.* 1981.

Wilson, Charles J. *The Indian Presence: Archeology of Sanibel, Captiva and Adjacent Islands in Pine Island Sound.* 1982.

FOR KNOWLEDGEABLE NATURALISTS

The following works are highly authoritative and, on the whole, not destined for a general audience of neophyte naturalists. However, I could not have written *Nature on Sanibel* without consulting such studies and benefiting from the vast knowledge of their authors.

Cooley, George R. "The Vegetation of Sanibel Island, Lee County, Florida," *Rhodora: Journal of the New England Botanical Club,* Vol. 57 (October, 1955), No. 682. Reprinted by the Sanibel-Captiva Conservation Foundation. A pioneering study of botanical life on Sanibel *before* development and the dominance of certain harmful exotics. Black-and-white photographs provide rare views of the island as it appeared in 1955. *Warning:* readers must be familiar with the Latin nomenclature for native vegetation.

Long, Robert W. and Lakela, Olga. *A Flora of Tropical Florida: A Manual of the Seed Plants of Southern Peninsular Florida.* Miami, Florida: Banyan Books, 1976. An extremely long and highly authoritative work. The bible for botanists in southern Florida.

Terres, John K. *The Audubon Society Encyclopedia of North American Birds.* New York: Alfred A. Knopf, 1980. Wonderfully detailed descriptions, not only of the birds themselves but of their habits as well. Far too heavy to carry around like a field guide, but well worth keeping in a bookcase for handy reference. The language is sometimes technical, but rarely impenetrable.

INDEX